Ten Studies in the Poetry of Matthew Arnold

Ten Studies

in the Poetry of Matthew Arnold

by PAULL F. BAUM

DUKE UNIVERSITY PRESS · Durham, N. C. · 1958

© 1958, Duke University Press

Library of Congress Catalogue Card Number
58 - 8499

Second printing, 1961

PRINTED AND BOUND IN THE UNITED STATES OF AMERICA
BY BOOK CRAFTSMEN ASSOCIATES, INC., NEW YORK

LECTORIBUS SINE NOMINE
DUOBUS
GRATO ANIMO
D D

This book was published with the assistance of the income from the P. HUBER HANES FUND.

Contents

Introduction

THE PUBLICATION in 1932 of Arnold's letter to Clough, followed in 1940 by the *Commentary* of Tinker and Lowry and by the *Poetical Works* from the same editors in 1950, has given students of Arnold's poetry a new impetus and a new security. And to these volumes must be added the massive *Essai de biographie psychologique* (with bibliography) by Professor Bonnerot in 1947.[1]

Arnold's poetry has always been appreciated and enjoyed by select readers, but it can hardly be called popular, and it has always seemed a little dry, and even artificial, to many. It separated itself from the main movement of popular Victorian poetry; it lacked the sunset glow of Romanticism by which Tennyson flourished (and inversely Browning) and by whose fading light Rossetti and Swinburne shone. It was limited in scope and in time. The first two volumes, 1849 and 1852,

[1] *The Letters of Matthew Arnold to Arthur Hugh Clough,* Edited with an Introductory Study by Howard Foster Lowry, London and New York, 1932; *The Poetry of Matthew Arnold: A Commentary,* by C. B. Tinker and H. F. Lowry, London and New York, 1940; *The Poetical Works of Matthew Arnold,* Edited by C. B. Tinker and H. F. Lowry, London and New York, 1950; Louis Bonnerot, *Matthew Arnold Poète: Essai de biographie psychologique,* Paris, 1947. These are cited below as, respectively, *Letters to Clough;* Tinker and Lowry, or simply *Commentary; Poetical Works;* and Bonnerot.

found few readers and with the Second Series of 1855 Arnold's career as a poet virtually ended. *Merope* in 1858 was like a knell. Of the *New Poems,* 1867, hardly half a dozen added to his stature; many of them were 'interesting,' but only 'Dover Beach,' and 'Thyrsis' were of the best, and they were not quite new in date of composition. Still it must be recognized that the various reprintings and re-editions, culminating in the posthumous Popular Edition in 1890, make an impressive list; and the *Selected Poems* of 1878 enjoyed ten reprintings. Arnold was even honored by a *Birthday Book* of selections, arranged by his daughter, in 1883. There must have been a body of the faithful, who admired and enjoyed.

Moreover, the magisterial *Essays,* largely controversial and on contemporary topics, and challenging (if the word is still admissible) even when they were about education or Homer or the de Guérins, made him a public figure, but for a time they overshadowed his poetry. There have been those who complained that the poet died in giving birth to the critic and who submitted their various reasons for this peculiar phenomenon. But now, when his critical work has been sifted and weighed, we have come more and more to recognize that on his poetry rests his real claim to immortality; and from this recognition must follow his belated revival in the new Victorian resurgence.

The limitation of this poetry, both in bulk and in scope, has been a handicap. His subjects were often intensely personal, even while he aimed at disinterested objectivity and deplored personal revelation; other subjects were remote from general interest—'The Church of Brou,' for example, the Obermann poems, 'Tristram and Iseult' and 'Balder Dead'—or he could not make them seem interesting. Often when we expect him to be at his best he falls short; there is a palpable failure, a notable element is lacking. This is especially true with those rich commonplaces so frequent among all worshipers of Apollo, which without a certain energy or delicacy of language become mere banalities, but which may sometimes mysteriously and unpredictably become poetry. On the other hand, so many of his poems have so many excellences that it is unfair to complain when he falls short of the *very best,* as he would say—unfair to seem to question them and likewise to take advantage of them for analytical dissection; unfair, until analysis reveals unsuspected values. His poetry has an air of deliberateness; he aimed at the grand manner, with its "simplicity" and "severity"—two most difficult qualities to achieve—and as a corollary it seems to want warmth, glow, passion.

Regarding one aspect of this poetry Arnold has never had his just deserts, his handling of meter. For example, a critic, with the weight of the English Men of Letters series behind him, could write:

The unrhymed lyrics are, to speak plainly, both here [in 'Emped-ocles'] and throughout this volume, detestable—

> *"Great qualities are trodden down,*
> *And littleness united*
> *Is become invincible."*

This is not poetry. It is scarcely even prose. It is something for which literature has no name.[2]

Perhaps the metrical experiments with trisyllabic feet in 'A Modern Sappho' and with strict trochaics in Part II of 'Tristram and Iseult' are unsatisfactory; but in other poems he has passages which are prosodically beyond praise. He employed a variety of conventional stanzas, often adorning them with subtle nuances. The ballad stanza occasionally betrayed him, as it has many others, into doggerel. With sheer music he succeeded only, but eminently, in 'The Forsaken Merman.'

[2] Herbert W. Paul, *Matthew Arnold,* London, 1902, p. 34.

His metrical contribution, besides the 'Scholar-Gipsy' stanza, was in the kind of chant he used first in 'The Strayed Reveller,' again in 'Consolation,' and with rime in parts of 'Bacchanalia.' This chant is indifferently iambic-trochaic. The staple line has two stresses, but expands to lines which are ambiguously two- or three-stress, and includes some lines with three (and rarely four) full stresses. For 'Rugby Chapel' he chose a modification of this: three-stress unrimed lines, predominantly trochaic. No one has managed these measures with such skill; they have the advantages of meter and much of the freedom of prose, and they never dwindle into singsong.

There is another aspect of Arnold's poetry which has been often overlooked. Frederic Harrison spoke up clearly in praise of its classical quality. "This balance, this lucidity, this Virgilian dignity and grace, may be said to be unfailing."[3] Beside those poems which may look like free improvising, there are many others which exhibit such careful workmanship, both phrasal and structural, that they verge on obscurity. They are classical in the sense that they require annotation. They are so *studied* that they become *difficult*. Such are 'In Utrumque Paratus' and 'Fragment of an "Antigone," ' both, like 'The Strayed Reveller,' in the 1849 volume. The first chorus in this Antigone 'Fragment' comes closer than anything else in English to reproducing the effect of compression, complexity, and weightiness of a chorus of Sophocles. It is not easy reading, but it rewards the effort it demands. This sort of 'challenge' Arnold both describes and illustrates in his epigram:

> *What poets feel not, when they make,*
> *A pleasure in creating,*
> *The world, in its turn, will not take*
> *Pleasure in contemplating.*

[3] Frederic Harrison, *Tennyson, Ruskin, Mill and Other Literary Estimates,* London, 1900, p. 106.

The unfailing "lucidity" claimed for Arnold by Frederic Harrison must be understood with a certain latitude. What often appears to be simple and lucid turns out, when examined attentively, to be sometimes surprisingly subtle and sometimes actually obscure. In either case, it craves the kind of interpretation only close analysis can give. It attests the "pleasure" which Arnold felt in "creating." Of the opposite sort is that early poem, 'The New Sirens,' which he revived, on Swinburne's urging (nearly thirty years after its first publication), with an apologetic note beginning: "I shall not, I hope, be supposed unconscious that in coherency and intelligibility the following poem leaves much to be desired." It was, he said, "a work produced in long-past days of ardour and emotion." One of his friends had advised "a running commentary" and for Clough, who had called it "a mumble," he provided one of over a thousand words. Here Arnold was his own commentor.

The invaluable work of Tinker and Lowry—not to mention the many others traceable in M. Bonnerot's bibliography—has not only opened the way for fuller appreciation and understanding of Arnold's poetry, it has also left lacunae to be filled and opportunity for 'expostulation and reply.' The following *Ten Studies* are in a way supplementary to their *Commentary:* occasionally they take issue, but more often they enlarge. The *Commentary,* moreover, has no place for textual analysis, but it has cleared the ground for the fully annotated edition, with illuminating help from the letters, which Arnold's poetry deserves—and towards which these *Studies* may serve as a contribution.

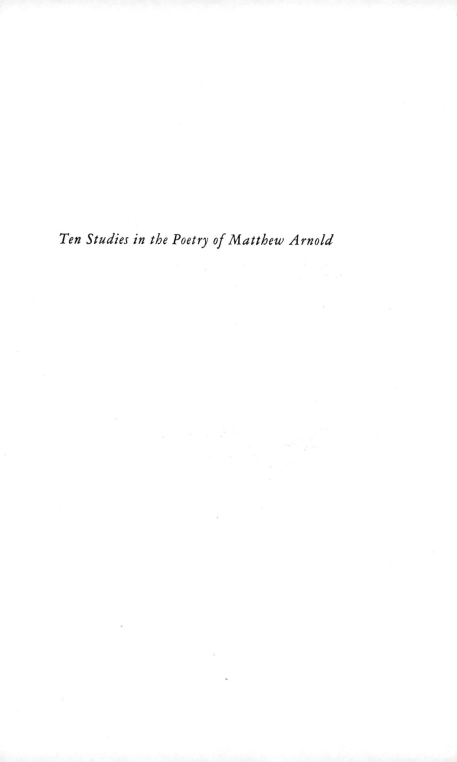

Ten Studies in the Poetry of Matthew Arnold

1. 'Shakespeare'

M ATTHEW ARNOLD's sonnet 'Shakespeare' has been generally admired but has not (apart from a few attempts in *Notes and Queries* and *The Explicator,* reviewed in n. 10) been subjected to exegetical scrutiny. No doubt many readers have thought they understood it, yet I have found, and still find, very serious differences of opinion among those whom I have consulted;—and so the way is open for a fresh attempt.

Three suggestions are offered by Tinker and Lowry. One is a letter of Arnold to Clough in December 1847 apropos of Clough's efforts "to *solve* the Universe": "I own that to *reconstruct* the Universe is not a satisfactory attempt either—I keep saying, Shakspeare, Shakspeare, you are as obscure as life is: yet this unsatisfactoriness goes against the poetic office in general: for this must I think certainly be its end." This might mean that Shakespeare's interpretation of life is as difficult to understand as life iteslf, and Shakespeare is accordingly unsatisfactory inasmuch as the end of poetry is to reconstruct the universe, and dramatic reconstruction does not make things any clearer. The sentence, "I keep saying, Shakspeare, Shakspeare, you are as obscure as life is," is regarded by Professor Lowry (p. 63, n. 2) as "really Arnold's own paraphrase of his sonnet." It may well be, if Professor Lowry is hinting that the sonnet is as obscure as Shakespeare himself, sometimes. But this does not help a great deal. The letter (which was written more than three years after the sonnet[1]) is also obscure.[2]

The second suggestion in Tinker and Lowry is based on a passage from the Yale MS (undated, but early), in which Arnold asks: What would Shakespeare say "at seeing his easy morality erected by Germans & others into a system of life"? And Arnold answers: "He would say—You fools—I have walked thro: life ἐπι ξυρου ακμης God knows how—if you mistake my razor edge, you damned pedants, for a bridge, a

---

[1] The sonnet "was first written out" in a letter to Arnold's sister Jane (Mrs. Humphry Ward, *A Writer's Recollections,* New York, 1918, 1. 52). One wishes that more about this letter were known, for the context might throw light on the sonnet itself. A MS of the sonnet, now in the British Museum, is dated 1 August 1844. Presumably the letter is earlier.

[2] Over against Clough's passion to *solve,* Arnold sets his own efforts (or perhaps only Shakespeare's) to *reconstruct* the universe. Both he finds unsatisfactory. Nevertheless, he believes that "the end" of "the poetic office in general" *is* to reconstruct the universe, unsatisfactory as must be any particular attempt to do so. Shakespeare himself, for example (he throws into a parenthesis), seems to be as obscure as life is.—One is hardly justified in pressing the language of such a letter too hard, yet the drift appears to be: Arnold has been irritated by Clough's way of solving human problems (by the direct didactic method and his emphasis on duty) and prefers his own way (of reconstructing the world by the dramatic method), which, he says, is the aim of poetry. But even this, the dramatic approach, is unsatisfactory; and it is a kind of reproach to the poetic function that one of the best poets has failed, or seemed to fail. Then Arnold adds, significantly, almost apologetically: "But have I been inside you, or Shakespeare? Never. Therefore heed me not. . . ." This qualifies the obscurity of Shakespeare in two ways: not only is it difficult to draw satisfactory conclusions from Shakespeare's dramatic representation of life, but also it is difficult, if not impossible, to penetrate the mind and therefore the ultimate meaning of any writer. Since the word *obscure* has this ambiguity, it is obviously not a word to conjure with; and accordingly Arnold's letter will help us but little in interpreting his sonnet unless we are careful to interpret correctly the letter also.

nice mess you will make of your own & others' walk & conversation."[3] This appears to mean that Arnold deprecates, for Shakespeare, the "easy morality" of the plays (or some of them) as a guide to modern conduct; that is, at the moment of writing this, Arnold seems to deny the cogency of Shakespeare's poetry for moral teaching. In that sense, perhaps, he thought that Shakespeare was "free" (from the responsibility of telling us how to live) and in that sense he was also obscure, because his plays offer no help at all for our own "walk & conversation." But neither of these is the natural meaning of "free" or of "obscure." There is a little more to this point, however, and I shall return to it later.

A third suggestion is offered by Tinker and Lowry in the possible parallel between the sonnet and Emerson's essay on 'Intellect.' At the close of this essay Emerson describes "the innocent serenity" of those "babe-like Jupiters" who "sit in their clouds, and from age to age prattle to each other and to no contemporary. Well assured that their speech is intelligible . . . without a moment's heed of the universal astonishment of the human race below, who do not comprehend their plainest argument. . . ." Certainly there is a superficial resemblance between this and part of the sonnet; and it is of curious interest as showing perhaps how a poet may transpose an idea for his own uses.[4]

[3] The Greek is from *Iliad* x, 173: ἐπὶ ξυροῦ ἵσταται ἀκμῆς, i.e., it stands on a razor's edge.

[4] Tinker and Lowry do not expressly say that the note in the Yale MS helps us to understand the sonnet. But they describe the Clough letter ("Shakspeare . . . as obscure as life is") as "In much the same vein"; and their quotation from Emerson about the unintelligibility of the language of philosophers implies an emphasis on Shakespeare's obscurity.—There may be also a reminiscence of Emerson in Arnold's 'Mycerinus,' on the aloofness of the gods. At Oxford Arnold read Emerson with enthusiasm: he was, along with Newman and Carlyle, one of the "voices"; and in his sonnet, 'Written in Emerson's Essays,'

The two statements of Arnold, then, that Shakespeare is obscure and that the morality of his plays affords no basis for a personal ethic, and the somewhat parallel matter from Emerson, may be taken as hints rather than helps. Is the sonnet any clearer?[5]

In the sonnet itself Arnold seems to say: Other poets submit to our questioning; Shakespeare is free from it, free in the sense that he does not "abide" it. We ask repeatedly—he smiles without replying. What, first of all, is the nature of this question? Three possibilities present themselves: the question of Shakespeare's rank or supremacy as a poet, the question whether his plays contain a revelation of his own

Arnold called him "A voice oracular." But in a letter to Clough (1853) he wrote of him as "very thin and ineffectual." In 1883, preparing for his lecture on Emerson, he reread the Essays, but on facing a New England audience he felt obliged to compromise. He denied Emerson a place among great writers and great philosophers, but compared him favorably with Marcus Aurelius—"his insight is admirable; his truth precious."

[5] One might hope to find further aid from Arnold's comments elsewhere on Shakespeare. (The references are conveniently collected by Lowry, *Letters to Clough,* p. 46, n. 1 and index.) But none of these overlaps with the apparent subject-matter of the sonnet. There may be a recollection of the second line in Arnold's Wordsworth essay (1879): "But one can imagine his smiling if one could meet him in the Elysian Fields and tell him" that he "frequently has lines and passages in a strain quite false." And in his review (1877) of Stopford Brooke's *A Primer of English Literature* there may be an echo of the mountain simile in the sonnet: "Mr. Stopford Brooke has remembered that Shakspeare is, as Goethe said, not truly seen when he is regarded as a great single mountain rising straight out of the plain . . ." (*Mixed Essays,* p. 144). This reference is to the *Gespräche mit Eckermann,* 2 January 1824. The context is of course different; it may be recalled, however, that Goethe in the same conversation said: "dass Shakespeare die ganze Menchennatur nach allen Richtungen hin und allen Tiefen und Höhen bereits erschöpft habe." This also is a commonplace, but something like it *may* appear in the last lines of the sonnet.

character and his private understanding of life (or more generally, perhaps, the whole question of how a creative artist works), and the question whether his plays may be regarded as providing us with a guide to conduct, a practical 'criticism of life' to be followed in our own emergencies. Perhaps Arnold meant none of these, so precisely phrased, but he must have meant something. These three possibilities, at any rate, may be pursued in turn, to see which leads to the most satisfying or likely result.

It is commonly agreed that Shakespeare as poet, perhaps also as playwright, towers above all the rest. There is no "question" about it, though we may ask about the relative position of other poets. Then in the first tercet Arnold adds that with all his superiority Shakespeare's genius was unrecognized during his lifetime (which is true in a general way); and then adds further that Shakespeare's poetry alone reveals all human sufferings: they

> *Find their sole speech in that victorious brow.*

But such an interpretation besides being forced seems rather trivial and implies a serious lack of unity in the sonnet. It may be dismissed at once.

It is true also that many have asked and asked about Shakespeare's private life and opinions; they have even scrutinized his plays for some supplement to our meager biographical knowledge of the poet, some autobiographical hints revealing 'the man.'[6] Others abide this questioning: they are

---

[6] Cf. Schiller's remark on Shakespeare, quoted by Bosanquet, *A History of Aesthetic* (London, 1934, p. 299): "Misled by my acquaintance with recent poetry so as in every work to look first for *the poet,* to meet him heart to heart, and to reflect with him upon his object, in short to look at the object only as it is reflected in the subject, I found it intolerable that here the poet never showed himself and would never let me question him."

provided with two-volume biographies and they reveal themselves in their verse. But not Shakespeare. He is, like the mountain summit, above such "foil'd searching."—No doubt something of this may be read into Arnold's sonnet; yet in this interpretation the significant phrase "out-topping knowledge" becomes nearly meaningless, or means only that Shakespeare's knowledge of himself goes beyond what we can ever obtain from the records or from his plays; and again the result is rather meager. Others find this view entirely satisfying. It has been suggested to me, for example, that Shakespeare's "out-topping knowledge" means that his personal life not only transcends our factual knowledge of him but also our desire for it and thus in a sense parallels Arnold's reproof of the Romantic poets for writing so much about themselves as well as his condemnation of those who advocated "a true allegory of the state of one's own mind" as "the highest thing that one can attempt in the way of poetry." Shakespeare had so 'schooled' himself and made himself so 'secure' against this confusion of his personality and his poetry that he could "tread on earth unguess'd at." He had endured the pains, weaknesses, and griefs of our mortality but left them out of his poetry; and his victory over them might be seen only in his serene "brow"— the brow of the lofty hill which uncrowns its majesty only to the stars.

Finally, is the question which other poets abide and Shakespeare does not, the question of moral teaching? Do the plays contain a helpful criticism of life? Opinions may differ on this point, but Arnold is certainly clear and explicit, in the negative sense, in the note already quoted from the Yale MS: the "Germans & others" are pedants and fools if they mistake "his easy morality" for "a system of life."[7] The sonnet is almost

[7] "Easy morality" is to be understood in the light of what precedes: "The easy tone of a Shakespeare suits the immoral-vulgar," i.e., the

equally clear and explicit: Shakespeare in his lofty communion with the stars and sunbeams refused—perhaps *disdained* is the word—to transmit his superior divine knowledge to mortals, refused to make his written work the expression of his own conscience.

The mountain simile[8] is presented with some detail. By the pronouns the "hill" is semi-personified to emphasize the comparison; i.e., Shakespeare "uncrowns his majesty" [only] to the stars,[9] he dwells in "the heaven of heavens" and exposes "but the cloudy border of his base" to the vain questioning of mortal men. Here, if we are to press the parallel, either of the two proposed explanations will fit: *either* Shakespeare has revealed his personality but cloudily to those who look for it as biography or as implicit in his plays, *or* he has deliberately not put into his poetry his own or any other system of life for "others' walk & conversation." Perhaps a combination of the two. (One may even extend this idea to include a moral detachment and a refusal to solve or reconstruct the universe.) It is noteworthy, moreover, that the octave of the sonnet and the first tercet are joined by the punctuation (in some texts a colon, in others a semicolon), so that the sense continues: as Shakespeare outtops humanity, dwelling with "the stars and sunbeams,"

---

groundlings like it; what is more, "the moralist conscious of his own imperfection & strain, admires it." This last is a somewhat darker saying.

[8] Note the canceled reading "So some sovran hill" for "For the loftiest hill." In 1869 Arnold wrote to Palgrave that he had "re-written" the sonnet (G. W. E. Russell, *Matthew Arnold*, New York, 1904, p. 43). The changes are recorded in the Oxford edition, 1950. They do not throw any helpful light on the meaning of the sonnet.

[9] The fifth line, "Planting his steadfast footsteps in the sea," seems to be pictorial rather than symbolic. It is a direct echo from Cowper (as noted by Tinker and Lowry), but also it suggests the full height of the mountain as seen rising from sea level to the stars.

Self-school'd, self-scann'd, self-honour'd, self-secure,

so his supremacy was unrecognized during his lifetime—
"Better so!"

There remains the second tercet, which is the most difficult
part of the sonnet and which may yield us the essential clue.
It is united with the first tercet by the rimes, yet seems to be
an independent statement:

> *All pains the immortal spirit must endure,*
> *All weakness which impairs, all griefs which bow,*
> *Find their sole speech in that victorious brow.*

This, at a simple and natural reading, ought to mean: all that
marks the strain and stress of Shakespeare's immortal spirit
living among men is visible only in his countenance, *videlicit,*
in a real or imagined portrait, but definitely not in the printed
works. For it would be a very forced metonymy which would
understand "victorious brow" as successful poetry springing
from the brain behind it,[10] and the three lines together as mean-

---

[10] Since this is the crux of nearly all interpretations, the previous
attempts may be reviewed here. Richard Hussey, in *Notes & Queries,*
18 April 1942, proposed tentatively: "You must have had pains, weaknesses and griefs; we know you overcame them; but their only record
is not in contemporary gossip but in your plays, we expect; instead of
which we seem to be fobbed off with the Stratford bust." In the 16 May
issue Wm. Jaggard said that Shakespeare's eminence was not unguessed
at, but simply unregistered by his contemporaries; he objected to the
phrase "fobbed off" and said Shakespeare was revealed both in the
Sonnets and in the portraits. In the same issue W. H. J. named the
Stratford effigy and the Droeshout portrait. Hussey replied, 20 June,
with the paraphrase of a friend: "Mortality searching the contours of
the mountain is foiled by the cloud-line. Shakespeare, whose mind
towered to the skies, was one whose greatness his fellows on earth
could not fathom. It was better so, because a mind, the capacity of
which can be gauged by contemporaries, must be limited by the ideas
and conventions of his age. But Shakespeare had that towering universal mind which could give utterance to all the emotions of the immortal spirit, the tragedies of weakness and sorrow. He alone could

ing that Shakespeare's poetry embodies all the sufferings of mortal men in this our mortal flesh. It would force the language and leave the sonnet with a striking but inappropriate conclusion. Nor is the case much improved if the "immortal spirit" is taken not as Shakespeare's but as mankind's: all of our sufferings find expression only in the lineaments of Shakespeare's face.

The sonnet is admittedly obscure and Arnold's skill is not above reproach. Others (it says) submit to our question— about what? The answer must be implied in that which

---

rise victorious above the cloud-line which bars the vision of mortal men." Hussey did not quite accept this, and added: "I always wanted the 'pains, weakness, griefs' to be those of the characters in the plays, not of the author. . . ." On 18 July A. E. D. voted for the Droeshout portrait and *not* the Stratford bust; and in the same issue Henry Pettit explained "victorious brow" as "the total achievement of Shakespeare." On 24 October Joseph E. Morris suggested that "victorious" referred to Shakespeare's victory over the dark period of his tragedies, and compared Arnold's sonnet 'To a Friend.'

Arnold's sonnet came in for discussion a few years later in *The Explicator*. In June 1946 Fred A. Dudley produced a "line-for-line" explication with interesting suggestions and summed up: "Other poets can be mastered; Shakespeare transcends all study as some great mountain (Everest?) rising . . . from the sea . . . above the limits of exploration. Reaching unaided the very peak of human achievement, he has never been fully understood; but in his pages. . . ." In December 1946 E. A. Philbrick opined that "abide" meant settle the question of Shakespeare's rank. In October 1947 E. M. Halliday (coming close to the view in the text above) took issue with Dudley; the loftiest hill refers to "the aloofness and independence of his personal life"; the question is "the private secrets of the soul" and Shakespeare "gives us almost no clues as to what he was or how he became it"; "far from 'unlocking his heart' . . . in his works or elsewhere, he reveals his calm triumph over private afflictions in the matchless serenity of his unfurrowed brow (as it is customarily represented in paintings and busts)." Finally, in the same issue, Carlton F. Wells also answered Dudley, saying that "sole" means unique, unrivaled, unmatched.—One may still add that the "paintings and busts" have little authority; they are at least one remove from the unfurrowed brow of Arnold's *imagination.*

follows. In spite of our continued asking Shakespeare silently smiles, "out-topping knowledge." We ask for knowledge, of whatever kind, and Shakespeare perhaps has it in abundance yet declines to impart it (or simply, is *above* knowledge). He is like a towering hill which we can know only at its cloudy base, where we mortals pursue our foiled search for truth—or possibly our search for the answers he declines to give. (This, it seems to me, is not a matter of Shakespeare's obscurity, which would imply inability to impart his knowledge; nor is it altogether a matter of practical morality, for the implication would then be that Shakespeare was rather artist than moralist: which is true enough but not what the sonnet says.) What the octave tries to convey, then, is that Shakespeare was superior to knowledge in our ordinary sense and not at all concerned with imparting it or sharing what he had. This fits also the sestet, which develops, with approval, Shakespeare's detachment from human life, and ends with the observation that the conflict between his humanity and the immortal spirit within him is visible *only* in his features, i.e., not in his plays. This gives the sonnet a general unity, and if it is not what we expected Arnold to say, the fault may possibly be our own.

The sonnet might be paraphrased as follows:

There is a kind of knowledge which others are willing to impart but which Shakespeare smilingly declines to impart though he has it,—or more accurately, transcends it. For he is like a great mountain: (1) *as* its summit is in the skies, (a) *so* his wisdom surpasses human knowledge; and *so* (b) he reveals his wisdom only to the stars; and (2) *as* mortals who dwell at its cloudy base are always seeking truth in vain, *so* we seek in vain to learn from his works (for he has left them clouded and obscure). Shakespeare is like the mountain-top [chiefly] in his aloofness from and independence of ordinary life; "unguess'd at," i.e., not known as he really was ("Have I been inside you, or Shakspeare? Never."). Yet he had to share it, and the sufferings of his immortal spirit here among

mortal men and his victory over them are known to us only from
his serene countenance.

The point is thus neither Shakespeare's obscurity nor the ethics
of his dramas, but his aloofness from the

> *Eternal mundane spectacle.*

For the best commentary on the sonnet and our best help in
understanding it is Arnold's own poem called 'Resignation,'
which was probably written at about the same time.[11]   There
his ideal poet is portrayed as holding aloof from mankind and
watching from his "high station" "that general life" unfold
without desiring to share its interests, affections, and "unreal
show." When 'Fausta' (who is the sister for whom the sonnet
"was first written out") objects that his poet "flees the common
life of men"—

> *He escapes thence, but we abide—*

and is therefore not a pattern for the rest of us, Arnold still
insists on "The poet's rapt security" and approves

> *His sad lucidity of soul.*

It is very like the sonnet.

[11] 'Resignation' was composed after the second walk across the
Cumberland fells, by tradition put in 1843, and before 1849, when it was
published. It will be recalled that the British Museum manuscript of
the sonnet is dated August 1844.

2. 'Mycerinus'

MANY READERS confess a weakness for 'Mycerinus.' It is of course a bravura show-piece, of a kind not now in fashion. It is rhetoric in the consciously grand manner, not quite so resounding as that of Almanzor, but better sustained than that of 'Laodamia.' It has none of the falsetto of

> *O terror! what hath she perceived? O joy!*

and it does not quite touch

> *The Gods approve*
> *The depth, and not the tumult, of the soul.*

But it has, along with a slightly similar situation, something of Wordsworth's eloquence without his frequent baldness. There is hardly a weak line in 'Mycerinus.' If Wordsworth could say of 'Laodamia': "it cost me more trouble than almost anything of equal length I have ever written," Arnold could probably have admitted a like labor; for no one produces so much smoothness—even Wordsworth did not—without sedulous use of the file. It has the air of being worked and reworked, to attain that *quiet* eloquence which has made Gray's 'Elegy' so memorable.

The parentage of 'Mycerinus' includes not only 'Laodamia' (first noted by John Duke Coleridge), whose stanza it employs

for the king's speech from the throne, but also Tennyson's
'Lotos-Eaters' (suggested by Tinker and Lowry) and notably
his 'Ulysses,' which it echoes in

> *It may be that sometimes . . .*
> *It may be on that joyless feast his eye . . .*
> *It may be;*

for Ulysses had warned his mariners

> *It may be that the gulfs will wash us down;*
> *It may be we shall touch the Happy Isles.*

There is in 'Mycerinus' something also of the "dull pomp, the
life of kings" which Ulysses leaves rather scornfully to his son
Telemachus. And Arnold's last line

> *Mix'd with the murmur of the moving Nile*

is a palpable imitation of

> *The moan of doves in immemorial elms,*
> *And murmuring of innumerable bees.*

Both are bad enough, but Arnold has the advantage of only
four *m*'s and one *n* against Tennyson's eight *m*'s and three *n*'s.
 The voice of Milton may also be heard, for as Mycerinus
wandered by the Nile

> *From palm-grove on to palm-grove, happy trees,*

Arnold must have recalled Syrian Rimmon, whose seat was

> *on the fertile banks*
> *Of Abbana and Pharphar, lucid streams.*

But

> *Six years—six little years—six drops of time*

and

> *While the deep-burnish'd foliage overhead*
> *Splinter'd the silver arrows of the moon*

and the golden cars that

> *through the mazy tracts of stars*
> *Sweep in the sounding stillness of the night*

are Arnold's own.

There is a kinship with 'Ulysses' not only in the formal farewell speeches of the two kings, but also in the total atmosphere of poetic magic, on different levels, which transcends a certain indifference to detail. 'Ulysses' is a little incoherent, though not to such an extent as Tennyson's other masterpiece, the 'Morte d'Arthur.'[1] Mycerinus makes himself a simile out of "yon star-shot ray,"

> *And turning, left them there; and with brief pause*

bent his way to the groves and wandered among the trees,

> *Their smooth tops shining sunward, and beneath*
> *Burying their unsunn'd stems in grass and flowers.*

It may be a quibble that flowers rarely grow without sun, but the transition from night to day is abrupt; and there seems to be a forced antithesis in

> *and ever, when the sun went down*
> *A hundred lamps beam'd in the* tranquil. *gloom,* . . .
> *Revealing all the* tumult *of the feast.*

Yet these are details compared with the reservation which Arnold introduced, puzzling nearly all readers.

i

Arnold took the 'story' from Herodotus, II, 129, 133. His Note, though in quotation marks, is not a quotation and is not "hastily summarized" (*Commentary*, p. 35) but is a selection of the elements of the story he had used. A straight translation

---

[1] Cf. Paull F. Baum, *Tennyson Sixty Years After*, Chapel Hill, 1948: pp. 299-303 for 'Ulysses,' and pp. 87-95 for 'Morte d'Arthur.'

of the passage in Herodotus might have misled a reader, for the purport of the incident as Herodotus tells it is that the king, while he had ruled his subjects with justice, was not above the impiety of trying to thwart the oracle and thereby negative the decree of fate. The moral which Arnold draws and for which the reader needed only the bare outline he 'quoted' is quite different.

In the first stanza Mycerinus sarcastically calls the oracle a "voice from lips that cannot lie" and that speak for the "powers of Destiny." He then talks generally of Gods and Powers and in stanza 7 a Power, altered later to Force;[2] and he questions whether these powers are indifferent to mortals, or are irresponsible, or merely aloof. This much was necessary to establish the attitude of the king: he had thought they were "all-just," now he repudiates them. But when he attempts to foil them by the trick of turning night into day—and living six years without sleep—something else intervenes.

Tinker and Lowry record the complaint "that the meaning of 'Mycerinus' is not clear, since the poet expresses no disapproval of the young king's abandonment of his duty, and seems to sympathize with the devotion of his six remaining years to revelry" (p. 36). This complaint misses the whole point; and so does their defense, comparing the "king's retirement from the world" with that of the Scholar-Gipsy and Arnold's own search for calm and self-knowledge. M. Bonnerot also has noted the biographical parallels (pp. 162-64). They are fairly obvious in the second stanza, and

> rapt in reverential awe,
> I sate obedient, in the fiery prime
> Of youth, self-govern'd, at the feet of Law

has its equivalent in the Grande Chartreuse 'Stanzas'

[2] The quotation " 'blind power' of the first edition" (*Commentary*. p. 37) is not justified by the variant readings in the 1950 edition.

For rigorous teachers seized my youth
And purged its faith, and trimm'd its fire.

One might almost see, albeit faintly, the Swiss encounter with Marguerite in the sixth stanza: "Man's common lure, life's pleasant things . . . joy in dances . . . Love, free to range." But the "double problème, intellectuel et moral" still lies elsewhere. To be sure, Arnold does not condemn or even suggest reproof of Mycerinus for leaving the throne to indulge in six years of idle ease and tumultuous feasting; nor was that form of escape either Matthew Arnold's or the Scholar-Gipsy's. The point is ironic, though the poem may not make it very clearly: that Mycerinus was justly angered and scornful of the ways of Destiny and justified in trying to thwart them; and lo, what seemed to be a false solution turned out to be salvation.

Sometimes, says Arnold, the king, after his abdication, while "loud joyful laughter" was on his lips, was startled by the thought of death and "on that joyless feast his eye" rested unseeing—"It may be," and so his soul

Was calm'd, ennobled, comforted, sustain'd.

The contradictory adjectives are purposeful and the paradox intentional. The trouble, if there is one, is not with the thought but with the expression. It was plain all along that Mycerinus was no roistering libertine and never could become one. His act was a mad rash protest against divine injustice, no doubt, and a foolish attempt to double his length of years; but he was "Girt with a band of revellers," never one of them. There is nothing in the text which says that he was really one of them except the mild statement that "he revelled night and day," that is, that he was with the revellers, not of them. He laughed with them, "but not less his brow was smooth" throughout the alternating seasons (very happily described), winter and summer, spring and autumn.

"It may be that sometimes" is a careful understatement—misleading if one reads it incautiously—coloring the whole description of the day-and-night revelry. The emphasis is on the king's reluctance to share it. The positive statement covers only a dozen lines, but in the rest it is implicit though indirect: "his mirth quail'd not . . . nor ebb'd . . . nor wither'd . . . nor grew dark" with the seasons. For while this seems to be explicit it implies the opposite: in spite of himself it did not quail, ebb, and so on. Even the word "mirth" is a calculated ambiguity: it includes the pretended revelry and the inner joy. Such is the feeling of the lines and of the whole second section of the poem. The moral thus is that Mycerinus, scorning the apparent injustice of fate, leaps from one horn of his dilemma to the other and paradoxically finds comfort where he had not expected it. The large movement is beautifully circular, to the surprise ("sometimes") of the reader as well as of the king. For Arnold to have said this bluntly would have destroyed his poem. We hear Mycerinus deliver his majestic sarcasms, see him proudly flee from the injustice of the gods and then discover that his wilfulness had brought an unforeseen but ennobling, sustaining reward; and we leave him with but distant echoes of the loud "mirth" subdued (with cunning effects of vowel and consonant) to "the murmur of the moving Nile." For Arnold has learned from Tennyson not only the prosodic trick but also the device of sudden expansion, or what is roughly called ending on a high note, which he used again and again later and most successfully at the end of 'Sohrab and Rustum.'

ii

The external form of the poem is also surprising: the shift from stanzas to blank verse. Evidently a contrast was intended, but one might have expected the dramatic speech to be in blank verse and the lyrical descriptive portion to be in stanzas. Yet one finds the rimed stanzas just right for the refined sarcasms of the formal speech and the blank verse right for the ironic sequel, especially since the blank verse is handled with its own peculiar originality. The last rimes are *praise* : *days;* the second line of the blank verse ends with *amaze;* and thereafter there is hardly a line which does not have, either near by or at some reasonable distance, its assonantal echo in vowel or consonant sound. In the whole number of forty-nine lines there are only ten scattered end words—*flower* (88), *joy* (90), *-head* (98), *lips* (101), *stems* (104), *strength* (109), *sustain'd* (111), *tranquillity* (115), *hall* (119), *flats* (126)—which do not fit into these interwoven sounds, and among these interwoven sounds there are three perfect rimes and one approximate rime. The effect, culminating in the studied two lines at the close, is very striking and the scheme must have been deliberate. I know of no parallels elsewhere in blank verse.

The full details are:—*scorn* (79) is an approximate rime to *on* (85). With *amaze* (80) there are echoes in *pause* (82) and then *trees* (86), *beneath* (87), *feast* (96). *Spake* (81) is followed by *way* (83) and much later by *day* (110, 122) and *days* (117). *Loved* (84) is echoed by *grove* (95). *Youth* (89) rimes with *reproof* (114), which is followed by *roof'd* (118) and which assonates with *smooth* (112); and in between are *gloom* (94, 113) and *moon* (99), preceded by *morn* (92) and *down* (93). *Tire* (91) and *wine* (97) anticipate *Nile* (127) at the end. Moreover, *morn* (92) and *moon* (99) are followed by *man* (102) and *man* by *mine* (106), *eye* (107), and *died* (116). *Shape* (103) is echoed by *came* (124), and *within* (108) by the rimes *spring* (120), *king* (125). *Soul* (100) rimes with *bowl* (105). *Clouds* (121) is echoed by *sound* (123).

3. 'Resignation'

R ESIGNATION,' the concluding poem of Arnold's first volume, has not found general favor in spite of some admirable lines and pasages. It was probably started in 1843, the year usually taken as the date of the walk and conversation recorded in it. "It is the kind of poem which somehow suggests repeated revision over a considerable length of time"; and it still seems to be a series of unamalgamated fragments. Indeed, Arnold's "youthful philosophy is not yet rigorously consistent, and perhaps not wholly clear to himself."[1] The poem requires therefore a careful examination to discover what senses Arnold attached to the word *resignation,* what autobiographical bearings the poem may have, and above all, how the different parts may be brought together into a kind of unity. For the prime difficulty is to find the necessary connectives. To Clough Arnold wrote in 1853: "How difficult it is to write prose: and why? because of the *articulations of the discourse:* one leaps over them in Poetry—places one thought cheek by jowl with another without introducing them and leaves them— but in prose this will not do. It is of course not right in poetry either—but we all do it. . . ."[2]

[1] Tinker and Lowry, pp. 63, 64, 67. For a brief summary of other criticisms of the poem see Bonnerot, p. 285. Bonnerot's own interpretation, by his *méthode intérieure,* is found on the following pages, 286-93.
[2] Ed. Lowry, p. 144.

i

According to the 'story' of the poem, Arnold and his sister, whom he calls Fausta, are at the top of the pass over the Cumberland fells, looking down towards Keswick, and he makes occasional use of the setting to illustrate his points. They are presumably about twenty years old. (In 1843 he was twenty-one and she twenty-two.) Apparently she has complained of unhappiness and a general discontent with her lot. "There are two kinds of people in this world," he begins, "first, those who have set themselves difficult tasks to perform and are ready to endure any hardships for the sake of ultimate success and the repose it will bring, but they would hardly venture to repeat their efforts; and, second, those who are less ambitious, who ask less of life, because they are naturally resigned to their circumstances or they have freed their minds of ambitious desires and therefore of the struggle necessary to fulfil them." He urges Fausta to be one of these latter.

She then recalls an excursion they have made as children with their father ten years before over the same country, and suggests that their ascent of the pass and weary but happy descent to the plains and seashore is a little like the experience of those ambitious people he has just described. She remarks that the country looks about the same as it did ten years ago, and that they themselves have not changed much either: in all this time we have done nothing with our lives. "We met earlier to-day," he goes on, "a band of gipsies who no doubt have been more than once, just as we now, over the same ground, and if they put their minds to it they would recognize the sameness with a feeling of dissatisfaction similar to yours. Life becomes a little harder for them every year, but they have learned to put up with it and somehow they will continue to put up with it until death releases them." He is thinking, perhaps, that the gipsies are like his unambitious people, resigned to their lot—which is not altogether a happy one—and implying that she might learn something from them.

Fausta makes no comment on this.

He continues then: "If you do not care to learn from the gipsies there are ways of facing the difficulties of life, viz., to overcome them by active effort for the sake of the rest at the end or to put up with them by patient endurance. There is, however, a third way, that of the Poet. The Poet is in many respects a superior being, with greater endowments than other men, but he does not devote his gifts to his own ends or satisfactions. He sees and understands the pride and ambition of others—but without envy. He never feels himself excluded from their pleasures—because he does not crave them. He looks as from a height on the various activities of mankind and these activities all melt into a distant vision of the long process of the ages. He sees not merely the present but the past and future, merging into one General Life whose object is continuance, whose aim is not individual happiness but peaceful existence. And there is an element of melancholy in this view which has to be recognized, this world being what it is."

Now Fausta speaks up. "I cannot accept," she says, "your analysis. Your gipsies are dull people, somewhat less than human, and therefore no model for me. Your poet, on the other hand, is so superior that I do not care for his rarified, abstract attitude. He may enjoy his comprehensive survey of the General Life; I even grant that he has a broad sympathetic feeling for the details of our existence; but he holds aloof from them, he escapes from them, he is not bound by the hampering confining circumstances which surround us ordinary mortals. His vision may be *wide,* but it is not *deep.* Your theories and your illustrations are all very well, but they do not apply to me."

"Very well, then," he replies, "I'll show you. You have to admit that these practical circumstances of our daily life— our personal desires, ambitions, and disappointments also—are all transitory. We come and go in our small way, but the world continues whether or no. That General Life on which the Poet concentrates his vision is the true reality, and the details, the personal interests of which you make so much, are but passing shadows, 'an unreal show.' Others have learned from *them* the vanity of human wishes. There is a compelling Fate which rules all things: the nearest we can come to an escape from it is by asking little from it, by drawing away from the changes and chances of the little world towards that same General Life, not even exposing ourselves to their power. This philosophy of withdrawal will be called weak and foolish by some, but not by Him who sees our small life as a mere moment in the universal flow of existence."

Fausta quietly points out, however: "Here we are in the midst of it, aren't we?—this troublesome terrestrial present."

And he answers finally: "Of course. But haven't I made myself clear? I admit that *this* life is a poor thing and *this* world an infected place; that Fate rules us here and we can do nothing about it. But such as it is, this life is bearable, and at the very least we can take example from these rocks and this lonely sky about us and suffer patiently, accept with resignation our present difficulties and hardships—what else is there? what better is there?—since you decline to entertain my larger view of acceptance, the Poet's view."

In brief: some people in this life are resigned in the sense that they will face any obstacle to achieve their ambition; others are just naturally resigned and accept what comes. These are the two extremes. But the Poet shows a different kind of resignation, that of rising superior to the circumstances of life, accepting them for what they are but not allowing himself to become involved in them. Since none of these views, however, fits Fausta, Arnold is driven to concede that ordinary life is a poor thing, mortals are at the mercy of a power they cannot control, and the only recourse is passive acceptance.

ii

Such is the main drift of the poem, its 'argument' rendered into simple prose. If this interpretation is accepted, several conclusions may be said to follow. First, the poem, though it may not have been conceived as a unit, must be allowed to have now, in its present form, a kind of unity, of progression from stage to stage, leading to a final position. In the course of the progression several forms of resignation are included. But they are treated not as steps in a logical argument, but rather as parts of a conversational discussion, in accordance with the outward plan of the poem, its structural setting. On the other hand, no little simplification was required in order to make this continuity of thought clear. In so far as the poem is regarded as the presentation of a philosophy of life— a critically unsound approach, but one evidently adopted by readers—Arnold is chargeable with a faulty method. For the pictorial adornments are sometimes out of proportion to their usefulness as illustration; the device of a conversation with his sister and the special circumstances of her 'case' are an inconvenience and to some degree a distraction.[3] Moreover,

[3] Some fifty years before this, Wordsworth revisited the Wye valley with his sister and in the famous 'Lines' talked things out with her, with somewhat of the same condescension, though to a quite different conclusion. The two poems have a few verbal and other parallels, as well as a similar structural dualism—when Wordsworth turns from the valley background and his concerns with the mystical ecstasy to thinking of his companion, and Arnold turns from the immediate situation to his generalizations on the Poet's escape from the pressures of daily life. In this respect Arnold's poem, despite its apparent fragmentation, achieves a better unity. But William's "exhortations" to Dorothy are quite unlike

the division of the material into distinct sections, many of
them with special marks of emphasis at the end, and the omission of the connectives, gives an impression of piece-work and
fragmentariness. And finally, the language, always highly
condensed, is often actually obscure.

Some of these faults are really the vices of the poem's
virtues. It is hardly arguable that Arnold has produced a far
from perfect work of art and a far from coherent statement of
the philosophy of resignation. The latter should not be required of him: all that we have a right to expect is a poetic
representation within the scope of his conversational scheme.
But when the artistic merits of the poem are canvassed, it will
appear that the pictorial elements are in themselves generally
successful: the Mecca pilgrims, the Crusaders, the Goths, and
the Huns; the topographical details of the Cumberland fells
are vivid and the description of the children's excursion done
with a proper lightness; the repetition of those details is skil-
fully handled; the picture of the gipsy campfire is wholly
admirable. And the reminiscent recurrence of various details,
now merely descriptive and now symbolic, is carefully managed
so as to give a general sense of unity. (The threefold picture
of the Poet looking down on human life is less successful because it contains a confused mixture of pictorial and reflective
elements.) Further, the allusions personal to the poet and his
sister, the actual circumstances of the two excursions, have their
own positive values, and may very well have seemed to Arnold
more attractive than he has made them for us; and may also
have seemed more promising as a method or plan for his poem
than they turned out to be in the execution. We can feel little
interest in Fausta's troubles except as she is a type of immature

---

Arnold's to Fausta, as Arnold's plea for the Poet's withdrawal from the
active life as a pattern for his own future is unlike William's recourse
to Nature as the nurse and guide of his moral being.

impatience and as she serves as a starting point of the poem. And the picture of her brother lecturing her is not altogether pleasant. But Arnold's own attitudes and judgments, particularly his conception of the poet's refusal to embroil himself in the affairs of ordinary men or the accomplishment of his own desires, *are* of some concern to us; and the poem thus makes its small contribution to biography.

All sorts of meaning may be interpreted into the poem. Arnold has been reading Lucretius and the Greek Stoics, and also the Bhagavad Gita. To Clough he wrote [1 March 1848]: "I am disappointed the Oriental wisdom, God grant it were mine, pleased you not. To the Greeks, foolishness." He had been reading Emerson, "A voice oracular," and wrote

> *The seeds of godlike power are in us still.*
> *Gods are we, bards, saints, heroes, if we will!*

only to add: "truth or mockery?" He doubtless knew Wordsworth's Prefaces and probably Goethe's *Wilhelm Meister* in Carlyle's translation. The early letters to Clough are full of his uncertainties about life and anxieties about himself. It is not necessary to ask if his idea of the Poet was based on Wordsworth or Goethe. If any particular poet, it may well have been Shakespeare, as he tries to represent him in the sonnet. The real subject of 'Resignation' is Arnold's own problem, his "conflict," his choice between the world and his own soul, the same question which had to be threshed out apropos of Marguerite and of Miss Wightman. Shall he devote his life to poetry? How does a poet live? (In the letter just quoted he told Clough: "My man [Lord Lansdowne] remarks that Poets should hold up their heads now a Poet [Lamartine] is at the head of France.") And so, under the guise of a conversation with Fausta, who is both Arnold's sister and Arnold himself, he argues the possibilities and ends, at this point, with the sad lucidity of a Stoic resignation. A few years later he made the great decision, and after that 'resignation' took on a different color.

iii

In view of the difficulties and obscurities of the poem a few attempts at detailed explication may be helpful.

1-39 The thematic introduction contrasting two types: the sternly and the mildly ambitious. Note the sixfold repetition of *So* and the fivefold rimes—*snows: rose,* and the triplet *propose: close: repose.* (There is another triplet 186-88.) Note also the spondaic lengthening of 21, with the consonantal pattern STST, as though to mark the close of the section. Besides this the rhetorical flourish in 85, the fine phrase at 198, and the alexandrine of 260 signal the section breaks. The pauses at 39, 107, 230 seem not to be so marked.

11-12 The *flooded plains* is one thing, through the flat sections of Hungary; the *groaning Danube* applies more properly to the gorge at Belgrade, the so-called Iron Gates.

17 It may be questioned whether the Crusaders looked for repose in the Holy Land.

21 *Past straits,* a double pun: past difficulties, and narrow passages passed through.

22-27 There are two kinds of mild natures: those who have achieved serenity by freeing themselves from the passions (by what method is not indicated), and those who are either born with a gift for resignation or have trained themselves for it. Both are subsumed in *These* (28). *These* in 25 refers to *passions.*

28-37 These who are resigned either by their nature or by self-discipline do not complain if their actions must conform to the daily situation. They are not like those others who want every step of their progress to be pleasant, accompanied by a *laughing Hour;* they do not ask that their progress be attended by favorable circumstances, or ask to be met, awaited, when they have come in their imperious advance through the cold and dark, and there to be escorted by these Hours with flaming torches for a certain distance—these Hours which (who) would thus be thwarted of their natural sweetness and laughter.—The difficulties lie in the double negative (these do not ask what the ambitious ask for, since they are not ambitious), and in the extreme condensation, the strained syntax, and the word order. But the pictures, once they are developed more clearly, are vivid and worth the effort.

38-39 *thou* may be Fausta, who is young and impatient, or Arnold himself. Fausta is usually *you* (40-214), but cf. 231 ff. The ambiguity is unimportant, since she turns out to be his *alter ego*. A little more than a year after this poem was published she was happily married to William E. Forster.

40-85 The excursion over the fells ten years ago. Canon Rawnsley, following family tradition, puts the first excursion in July 1830 (others 1833). Dr. Arnold (who was born in the same year as Carlyle and Keats) would have been thirty-five (or thirty-eight). The others were K (Fausta), Tom and Matt Arnold, and Captain Thomas Hamilton (see E. K. Chambers, *Matthew Arnold, A Study,* Oxford, 1927, pp. 41 f.). The crippled landlord was John Hawkrigg. (Cf. H. D. Rawnsley, *Literary Associations of the English Lakes,* 1894, 1901, 11, 216-18.) Chambers (pp. 41-43) would put the two walks in 1838 and 1848. None of the evidence for the dates is quite convincing. Arnold's note says that those who are familiar with the district will recognize the inn and its "sedentary" landlord at Wythburn, "and the passage over the Wythburn Fells to Watendlath." But this is not the whole story. The details of the text are picturesque rather than topographically satisfying. The climb from Wythburn to the top of the ridge is c. 1000 ft. and the descent to Watendlath c. 800 ft.; the *motley band* may well have had a *serious air* and have lingered towards the end. The *brook* (76) is the Watendlath and the *noisy town* is Keswick (pop. c. 4000 in the thirties and forties, but its cobblestones make it noisy). The brook however does not take them to Keswick, only to the southern end of Derwent Water and the Falls of Lodore (not mentioned!); it is 2-3 miles farther to the town. From Keswick they probably drove to Cockermouth (Wordsworth's birthplace) and on to Whitehaven (*the sea*), or "presumably at Maryport," says Chambers, some twenty-five more miles. The text is carefully noncommittal. Those readers who look for allegory and symbol will find them easily in the river of life, the dusty road, the noisy town, the sea of life, and so on. The eager young walkers are not unlike the Mecca pilgrims, Crusaders, Goths, and Huns,

> *Whom labours, self-ordain'd, enthrall.*

They would have welcomed the repose *That night.*

60-63 parenthetical: the party as seen by others from a distance. The *wavering, many-colour'd line* (*motley bands,* 45) implies a larger number than in the first recorded journey, but the increase may be put down to poetic hyperbole. The picture resembles the *struggling files* of Crusaders (6); it also reappears in 'Rugby Chapel,' 171-73, 205:

> *See! In the rocks of the world*
> *Marches the host of mankind,*
> *A feeble, wavering line . . .*
> *Strengthen the wavering line.*

Similarly the Alpine snows which *eddying rose* over the Goths (8) reappears as the avalanche in 'Rugby Chapel,' 123. In fact "the course of the life Of mortal men on the earth" ('Rugby Chapel,' 58 ff.)—those who strive towards "a clear-purposed goal," those who falter, and those who win through the storm, etc., with Dr. Arnold vaguely as their leader ("A God Marshall'd them")—is something like a replica of the young travelers over the Cumberland fells in 1830 or 1833.

86-107 The same scene on the fells, now revisited.

89 *ghosts* is echoed in 123. Dr. Arnold died in 1842.

108-43 The gipsies they have just met have also been here before, but in spite of their troubles they keep going. They also, like you (us) might *if they would,* i.e., if they reflected on the monotony of their lives, feel disquieted. Fausta may learn something from their patience and endurance.

113 *migratory race:* eighteenth-century style, in contrast to the colloquialisms in 132, 138, 182. Cf. also "preferment's door" in 'The Scholar-Gipsy,' 35.

118 Metrically suggestive of the picture.

130 Their blood runs thinner but the March wind is no less bitter.

144-98 The change of subject is abrupt, without transitional help, except for *quicker,* which may perhaps refer to the gipsies (the Poet is more sensitive than they are), but more naturally to all who are not poets, and even specifically to Arnold and Fausta in the poem. A few details resemble Wordsworth's 1800 Preface: a poet is one who is "endowed with more lively sensibility, more enthusiasm and tenderness, who has a greater knowledge of human nature, and a more comprehensive soul, than are supposed to be common among mankind."

148 *he* is ambiguous: man or poet, but evidently the latter, though moving mountains and loosing chains are not customary with poets. But 153 explains the paradox. *He* in the next line adds the necessary correction: a life of action in the world is not a Poet's life; his life is one of aloof, contented contemplation of human affairs; he looks without envy on those who rule in high places, nor does he crave beautiful women. Perhaps Arnold had Lamartine in mind, who was Minister of Foreign Affairs in 1848; or Shelley with his real and imaginary loves and his conception of poets as the "unacknowledged legislators" of this world.

154 ff. He *sees* in memory or in imagination . . . ; but 160-63 may be taken more literally; then 164-69 is generalized, but with an echo of 92-93; 170-84 is again realistic (remotely suggesting Fox How, or 'The Youth of Man,' 61-87, where the setting seems to be Laleham); finally the pictures return to the imaginative. In the morning the Poet, leaning on his gate, enjoys the beauties of nature and watches the shepherds set forth; but what he really sees is not the single view but its continual repetitions— the *continuous* life of mankind whose *dumb wish,* as he recognizes with a *sad lucidity,* is *not joy, but peace.* Cf. *243-44.*

189-90 clearly echoes 94-95. Here, says M. Bonnerot (p. 292), the tonality modulates from major to minor. "Le poème aurait pu s'arrêter là, car cette note est en somme une conclusion suffisante."

199-214 Fausta repudiates for herself the example of the gipsies, and both for herself and for all men (*but we abide*) the example of the Poet. Arnold had not recommended the aloofness of the Poet for all men, but he lets her objection pass in silence.

206-14 Deeper the Poet feels ... Not deep the Poet sees. This is neither a paradox nor a contradiction, but rather a want of clarity in Arnold's language, due to condensation. Fausta recognizes that the Poet feels a deep sympathy for the human lot, but he withdraws, escapes from the diurnal perplexities which afflict her. The Poet has a breadth of vision, yes, but he does not see deeply enough into the individual's problems to be of any help to her burning heart; he sees only, thinks only of *That general life* which has no appeal for her. Arnold's reply that the general life of the *world* transcends the affections and passions of the individual still does not satisfy her, so he retreats to a secondary position, begging her not to condemn the Poet's view, though she may not be able to share it.

215-30 The *world* transcends mankind's special interests—and even if these interests were widened beyond the merely human, there would still be farther regions of *eternal change.* One might expect 'changelessness,' regions of infinite calm and peace beyond our human passions. But Arnold must mean that the universe, if we could know it, is in eternal flux—a region without comfort and without peace.

230 *In some sense* is an odd qualifying phrase, but Arnold means that as our personal affections are trivial compared with the world's affairs, so also is the death of any one of us.

231-60 Summary restatement: renunciation of personal desires in favor of the Poet's freedom and security.

231 *thou,* Fausta or Arnold himself; both. So also 239, 241. But in 245 *thee* is Fausta only.—*him,* Arnold and/or the Poet. See note on 38-39.

235 Cf. 148-63.

243-44 fit Arnold's own predicament in the late 1840's.

245-48 Here is the chief statement of the poem's sense of *resignation.* Fate may refuse us, both of us, the *rapt security* of the Poet, but still we can overcome fate by asking nothing of chance, by being reconciled to what we have and are. In this way, he adds, we can all *Draw homeward to the general life,* that is, escape (like the Poet) from the snares of *individual strife.*—This is of course the language of argument rather than logic.

253-54 Again highly condensed. Those who retreat from *men's business* as a first step towards the higher view resemble un-opened leaves: they have not yet matured in the full sun of the Poet's lofty detachment. They may look foolish to the so-called *wise* (the Greeks? see the letter to Clough quoted above); they may seem weak in the world's eye, yet not *in His eye. . . .* Here the capital H must be an intentional ambiguity: surely not the Poet's eye and not quite God's, in the biblical sense. In succes-sive editions Arnold frequently altered the capitalization, but never this one. The early editions capitalized *Poet* and were followed by the Oxford University Press edition of 1909 *et sqq.;* and I have followed them here to distinguish Arnold's ideal figure from just any poet. But the Macmillan (Popular) edition of 1890 *et sqq.* and the Oxford edition of Tinker and Lowry, 1950, has *poet* throughout this poem.

261-78 Probably the most difficult passage; cf. p. 24 above.—If this our ordinary life seems hardly worth while, still these natural phenomena all about us now seem to *bear, forbear* (accept things with resignation) rather than *rejoice* (feel happy about them). And even if men's complaints and prayers for a fuller life could reach the ear of Fate, still the *general* situation *is* (one expects 'would be') not improved because we have forgotten in our zeal for action how wretched a place the world is. The first sentence (261-70) is intelligible: let us learn resignation from nature. The second sentence (271-78) is baffling. It appears to say: even if our prayers for a better life in this world should be answered, things would not be improved, because the world is what it is, somehow bad. This is certainly resignation at its most abject, all hope abandoned; whereas there might have been a note of consolation for Fausta and a thin note of consolation for all of us as the reward of being resigned. But this is not all; further expansion is needed. Even if (says Arnold) with our perpetual prayers we could prevail over Fate, the lot of mortals would be no better—and we cannot prevail over Fate, therefore the lot *is* no better. In short, the appeal to Fate is vain. Why? *Because* in our zeal for action we forget (we are made to forget) that very thing which makes the *world* bad. The world is the scene of our "diseas'd unrest," the "fool passion" which deceives us,

Call it ambition, or remorse, or love,

the "gradual furnace" which consumes or hardens our spirits ('Tristram and Iseult,' III, 112 ff.):—this *world* in Arnold's sense here, the world from which the Poet escapes, is infected by our own demand for *action*. To repeat: the appeal to Fate is vain *Because*—and now this word becomes a logical stumbling block. What he means is: There is no point in appealing to Fate because our troubles are of our own making. We beseech Fate to relieve us of the burden we have ourselves created. We make the world what it is and therefore it is unreasonable, *intemperate,* to pray to Fate about it. It is foolish to complain of Fate, when we are the real cause of our complaints.—Whether this is the right, the best conclusion for the poem, or not, it is in harmony with the general tenor. Ambition, too much concern for one's personal aims, should be resigned in favor of something higher; the Poet is a model in this regard; and if we are now dissatisfied, the blame should rest where it belongs, on us. *We* is both Fausta and Matthew Arnold. But Fausta is only a decoy; the real subject of the poem is Arnold's choice between the world, the flesh (Marguerite and presently Miss Wightman), and the devil (a remunerative post) on the one hand and on the other his ambition—this is the submerged corollary—to devote his life to poetry, to succeed as a Poet.

4. 'Tristram and Iseult'[1]

T RISTRAM AND ISEULT' has had few admirers either at the time it was first published (1849) or more recently, when the story has become familiar. Arnold himself, though he reprinted it, with revisions, in successive editions of his poems, admitted a dissatisfaction with it. The reasons for his failure with so fine a subject, an "action" from which, in his own words, a poet should receive "interest and force," are not difficult to undersand. I shall try to suggest them incidentally in the following paragraphs. But criticism of the poem has

[1] This study is in the main an examination of Arnold's incomplete and ambiguous statements regarding his sources for the Tristram poem, and of the incomplete and unsatisfactory discussion of them by Tinker and Lowry (*Commentary*, pp. 106-24). It presupposes an acquaintance with their pages and accordingly omits the formal references to their material. The two articles by la Villemarqué ("Les poèmes Gallois," in *Revue de Paris*, 1841, and "Visite au tombeau de Merlin," in *Revue de Paris*, 1837) and the article by Louandre ("L'Enchanteur Merlin," in *Revue de Paris*, 1840) were first identified by Lowry (*Letters to Clough*, p. 137, n. 3). The letter to Herbert Hill, of which only parts are quoted in the *Commentary* (pp. 109, 124), was first published in *T.L.S.*, 19 May 1932. Arnold gives the first of the three French articles as his primary source, but does not mention the other two. He says also that later he used Malory. In the second printing of the poem he gave an extract from Dunlop. I have attempted to unravel his uses of all these as clearly as possible and then added some general comments.

been made particularly difficult both by the confusing statements of Arnold regarding his 'sources' and by certain hasty
judgments resulting from what appears to be a misunderstanding of the evidence. It is these latter which I wish now to
consider.

i

In any critique of this poem a study of the sources is more
than ordinarily important. It is obvious that Arnold missed
the essential tragic import of the Tristram and Iseult story as
we now see it: the tragedy of an overmastering passion, "puri-
fied by suffering and as it were consecrated by death," in which
love transcends all other human relations and in which the
lovers are innocent victims of a well-intentioned but accidental-
ly misappropriated magic philtre. But without examining the
circumstances, it would be unsound to charge Arnold with
failure to recognize and use the story as high tragedy, just as
it would be wrong to credit him with a novel treatment of
familiar material. His treatment is closer to domestic tragedy
than to a *drame passionel,* and the critical problem is to discover why.

We have two statements from Arnold regarding his source.
In a letter to Herbert Hill, dated 5 November 1852, he said:

I read the story of Tristram and Iseult some years ago at Thun in an
article in a French Review on the romance literature: I had never
met with it before, and it fastened upon me: when I got back to
England I looked at the Morte d'Arthur and took what I could,
but the poem was in the main formed, and I could not well disturb
it. If I had read the story first in the Morte d'Arthur I should have
managed it differently.

And in a letter to Clough, dated 1 May 1853, he said:

my version of Tristram and Iseult comes from an article in the
Revue de Paris, on Fauriel, I think: the story of Merlin is im-

ported from the Morte d'Arthur. If I republish that poem I shall try to make it more intelligible. . . . The whole affair is by no means thoroughly successful.

But there is another possible source of Arnold's Tristram material, though it must be understood that Arnold never (so far as the available evidence goes) gave it as a source, namely, Dunlop's *History of Prose Fiction*. It will be recalled that when the poem first appeared more than one reader complained of the difficulty in following the story, which was of course unfamiliar to English readers at that time;[2] and apropos Arnold wrote to Clough in August 1853 that Froude had recommended "prefacing Tristram and Iseult with an extract from Dunlop's Hist. of fiction to tell the story, in preference to telling it in my own words." Accordingly, in the second edition, 1853, Arnold printed as a Note a much abbreviated *rifacimento*, in quotation marks, of Dunlop's version of the story. One may infer from this procedure only that Arnold was indebted to Froude for the suggestion that he use Dunlop as a convenience, and perhaps as testimony of the antecedent history of the tale; or that Arnold first learned of Dunlop's *History* from Froude after his poem was published and therefore cannot have used it as a source. Certainly there is no necessary inference from the letter to Clough that Arnold did use Dunlop as a source, and whatever evidence there may be must be internal evidence, that of the poem itself. It would thus not be correct to assume that Arnold had read Dunlop while he was at work on the poem. This being the case, it is both reasonable and methodologically proper to observe first what elements of Arnold's poem derive naturally from the French article (on which the poem was "in the main formed");

[2] This complaint is implied in Arnold's letter to Clough already quoted; it is explicit in Clough's review of the volume in *North American Review*, LXXVII (July 1853), 1-30.

second, to observe what elements were taken from Malory after Arnold's return to England; and third, only after due recognition of Arnold's own imaginative additions, to see if any elements of the story as Arnold gives it can be traced to Dunlop alone. That is, if anything remains unaccounted for in the *stated* sources which is not easily attributable to Arnold's creative imagination and yet is in Dunlop, such must be presumptive evidence that Dunlop is one of the sources, though Arnold never named him as such.

ii

Thus the starting point for an examination of Arnold's sources for 'Tristram and Iseult' must be his statements to Hill and Clough that he became acquainted with the story at Thun (probably in 1848 or 1849), in the article on Fauriel in the *Revue de Paris,* and that when he looked further in the *Morte d'Arthur* the poem as he conceived it was too fully "formed" for him to alter it greatly. There is no evidence, however, for or against the possibility that he had written anything down before he read Malory. After this, one should note what in the finished poem is not in the French article and is in the *Morte,* and therefore what presumably Arnold added to his material after he returned to England. Then if the Malory material appears to be so clearly interwoven with the *Revue de Paris* material as to preclude simple additions, it may safely be inferred that none or very little of the poem was already written—as distinct from "formed"—before he consulted Malory.

When the outline of the story as Arnold found it in the article by la Villemarqué is considered in relation to the published poem, it would seem that Arnold conceived the story as one of two contrasting loves represented by the two heroines, with special sympathy for the Breton Iseult, who suffered most from Tristram's divided loyalties. Tristram's tragic conflict, as we are accustomed to see it—the tragedy of an overpowering passion, thwarted by circumstance and brought to a solution only by death—has apparently not appealed to him or touched his imagination; least of all had he felt what we most feel. In those 'criticism of life' verses (Part III, 112-50) which he withdrew from the second and third editions and restored in the fourth, he complained:

How this fool passion gulls men potently

with no slightest hint of sympathy with the two lovers. And the whole of Part II is pitched in a querulous, almost truculent key. Iseult of Ireland interested him mainly as a foil to the other Iseult. From beginning to end the poem is her poem, the Breton Iseult's; and so he must have reconstructed the story he read in la Villemarqué and on this simple outline, strengthened later, after he had seen Malory, he let his imagination play freely.[3] Tristram returns from Ireland with Iseult, they drink the magic potion, she is married to Mark but continues to love Tristram, their liaison is discovered, he flees to Brittany and marries the other Iseult though still faithful at heart to his first love and seeks forgetfulness in knightly adventures, in the course of which he receives a mortal wound; he is tenderly nursed by his wife, sends for Iseult of Ireland, and dies just as she comes to him. They are buried together, leaving Iseult of the White Hands to live on, devoted to their two children.

[3] It seems likely, though not demonstrable, that Arnold's conception of the two Iseults is his own. They afford a striking and necessary contrast to set off the two great episodes of Tristram's career. Arnold's sympathies must have been with the Breton Iseult from the start; and he would later have found partial confirmation in Malory, who describes her as "both good and fair and a woman of noble blood and fame" (VIII, xxxvi). But Malory goes on to say that the marriage was not consummated, and *this* Arnold could not accept.

It is curious how much of la Villemarqué's bare summary Arnold discards: the battle with Morhoult in Cornwall, the poisoned dart, the first meeting with Iseult in Ireland, and Tristram's return to Cornwall with praise of her to his uncle. He omits mention of Brangien, and of King Houel later; he condenses various details of the liaison, discovery and reconciliation with March, passes over the trial by oath, with the incident of Tristram disguised as a beggar, and Tristram's battles against the knights of the Round Table; and noticeably says nothing of the second Iseult's jealousy and her representing that the Queen of Cornwall has refused to come to him, so that Tristram dies of *chagrin*. These omissions are obviously in the interest of simplification of Tristram's early life, with corresponding opportunity to keep the attention on his last days.[4]

What Arnold does with this bare outline is striking enough. He invents the death-bed scene with the Page[5] in which Tristram in delirium recalls two vivid incidents of his life with Iseult of Ireland and two other incidents illustrating his haunting memories of her after his marriage, and a final scene in which Tristram tenderly bids goodnight to his watching wife. To make these six passages, the longest of which is but seventeen lines, clear to the reader and to fill in supplementary or explanatory details Arnold uses a Breton bard (never so named, however) as narrator and commentator, who speaks in a dif-

[4] The harsh treatment of Brangien, which so shocked Dunlop, is not in la Villemarqué and therefore was not "omitted" by Arnold (*Commentary*, p. 107).

[5] La Villemarqué prints (pp. 275 ff.) the translation of a Welsh poem in dialogue between Tristram and Goualmai (Gawain) describing an incident in which Arthur has sent Gawain with twenty-eight men to persuade Tristram to return to Arthur's court. It is possible that this suggested to Arnold the dramatic form for the opening of his poem. La Villemarqué notes, moreover, that the poet "a laissé un curieux dialogue où il prend l'histoire *in medias res*."

ferent meter: variations of the short couplet. Whatever one
may think of Arnold's success in these explanatory passages
(which comprise 307 out of 373 lines of Part I) his general
plan can only be admired. By commencing with Tristram's
death he aimed to subordinate the early life of his hero with
Mark and the Queen,—only to be snared by the difficulty of
reducing the rich variety of incident which *is* the main story
and to be exposed to dangers of disunity of effect. His first
readers, moreover, unfamiliar even with the bare outline of the
story which Arnold knew, revealed to Arnold the double risk of
his strategy: there was both too much and too little explanation. The scheme was excellent, the execution deficient.

Part II, the death of both Tristram and Iseult, with the
lines which follow,[6] and Part III, the "young surviving Iseult"

---

[6] The passage, II, 101-93, has its own special interests, besides the numerous textual alterations.—After the death scene, in trochaic quatrains,
the meter and narrative method of Part I are resumed, with the 'Breton
bard' describing Iseult in death and a "ghostlike tapestry" on the wall
of the room. But the narrator, who had formerly seemed to be present
at the bedside of the dying hero, now speaks of the lovers as having died
"A thousand years ago."—In 1852, when 'Tristram and Iseult' was first
published, it was immediately preceded by a poem called 'Lines Written
by a Death-Bed.' The latter portion of these 'Lines' was probably an
independent poem, dated December 1851 (*Commentary,* p. 43)—after-
wards associated with the quite perfect 'Requiescat,' first published in
1853—and was reprinted under the title 'Youth and Calm' in *New
Poems,* 1867. Then in 1869 Arnold inserted in the original version of
'Tristram and Iseult' the first portion of the 'Lines' (now Part II, 131-46),
with the change of "youngest rival" to "younger rival." Much later
(and first as a MS alteration in his copy of the New Edition, 1881) he
made the more significant change of "curtains hid her face" to "bed-
clothes hid her face." Thus what had first of all been two separate
poems were joined together and published as one in 1852; then one of
them was reprinted in 1867 with a new title and in 1869 the other was
transferred to 'Tristram and Iseult.'—The "ghostlike tapestry" represents
a hunter with his dogs in a forest staring into the room where Tristram
and Iseult lie dead and seeming to say to himself: Where am I? Who are
the Knight and the Lady? "By a daring invention of the poet," says

and her children, are almost entirely Arnold's invention—except of course the closing Merlin and Vivian story. It is therefore necessary to examine closely the details of Part I to see what Arnold has done with his sources, especially to distinguish the elements which he took from Malory. But first a few matters not in any of the sources should be noted. He gives Tristram brown hair, Iseult of Ireland dark eyes and·raven hair, and Iseult of the White Hands golden hair. He adds that she is an orphan, whereas both la Villemarqué and Malory mention her father, and Malory also her brother;[7] and generally he lays stress on the pathos of her position. Arnold adds her two children, nowhere mentioned in any other version, for the sake of the domestic touches in Part I and in preparation for Part III. His characterization of the Irish Iseult as proud and petulant is likewise his own, to point the contrast with her long-suffering "rival." He describes Tristram as skilled in harping, as in la Villemarqué, and also in hunting, as in Malory. At I, 129 he says that Iseult left Ireland "at her father's will." This is directly from Malory (Book VIII, chap. xxiv) where King Anguish even urges Tristram to marry her himself instead of handing her over to King Mark. La Villemarqué

---

the *Commentary* (p. 114) this hunter in the arras is Tristram. Perhaps. But if he *were* Tristram, why, unless in heavy irony, should he pretend not to recognize his Iseult and himself? It is more likely that the tapestry speaker is another example, like the Tyrian trader at the end of 'The Scholar-Gipsy' and the children of the abbey at the end of the Grande Chartreuse 'Stanzas,' of Arnold's way of rising to a climax by means of a new and unrelated picture.

[7] So far as I have found Malory nowhere mentions the death of King Howel. Dunlop (4th ed., London, 1876, p. 86) has: "Runalen, brother of the white-handed Yseult, who had lately succeeded his father in the duchy of Britany," just before the escapade in which Tristram receives his mortal wound. This is the nearest we come to any indebtedness to Dunlop (except in the instance to be noted below); but it is more likely that Arnold made her an orphan simply to enhance the pathos.

says little of the voyage from Ireland to Cornwall, and Malory very little, except to relate the drinking of the love potion. But Arnold emphasizes it (lines 56-160 *passim*): the time is May and they see the "green fields of Wales" from their ship. Malory, however, describes their adventure at the Weeping Castle (VIII, xxiv-xxvi) and in his next chapter (xxvii) the meeting with Sir Galahad "in these marches"; after which "Sir Tristram and La Beale Isoud went to sea and came into Cornwall" (xxviii). The mention of Wales would be natural, but Arnold may have taken a hint here from Malory; and he may well have recalled a later chapter (VIII, xxxviii) in which Tristram and his Breton wife were driven by the wind "in to the coast of Wales upon this Isle of Servage."

All the accounts of the love philtre differ in detail. Arnold has Iseult ask for the "golden phial" and Tristram drink from it first (lines 100 f. and 145 ff.); and to make this clearer he added in the second edition lines 56-82 with an explanation of the "spiced magic draught" and its effect; and in the following section he alludes again to it, calling it a "potion rare" which her mother had given her. La Villemarqué says it was given to Brangien and that Tristram "par mégarde" drank it and gave it to Yseult. Malory is more circumstantial, relating that her mother gave it to Dame Brangwaine and to Gouvernail, Tristram's man (neither of whom does Arnold mention), and that on the voyage Tristram and Isoud "were thirsty, and they saw a little flacket of gold stand by them, and it seemed by the colour and the taste that it was a noble wine"—one which Brangwaine and Gouvernail were keeping for themselves (xxiv).[8] Arnold's account is simpler than Malory's, as usual, and he need have taken nothing from Malory here.

[8] Much the same is in a quotation by la Villemarqué (p. 278; not in Tinker and Lowry): "Tristan, accablé de chaleur et de soif, le prit

The last meeting of the two lovers in Cornwall is Arnold's condensation into a single scene of what la Villemarqué represents as going on for several years—an artistic advantage and almost a necessity for Arnold's summary treatment of the long story. But even here he adds imaginative touches of his own— the "pleasaunce-walks" and the rather anachronistic "winter-parlour"—further developed by the Breton commentator. The extended account in Malory, with its manifold incidents and digressions, was of no use to him.

On Tristram's reasons for leaving Cornwall after the innocence of Iseult has been established by a trick, la Villemarqué's précis says nothing: merely "il se retire dans la Petite-Bretagne." Malory of course is fuller; Mark has found Sir Tristram and La Beale Isoud together in a manor and carried her off home, but Isoud sends a message to Tristram, who is suffering from the wound of an empoisoned arrow: "she biddeth you haste into Brittany to King Howel, and there ye shall find his daughter, Isoud La Blanche Mains, and she shall help thee" (VIII, xxxv). Arnold seems to have taken a little of this—

> *The press'd fugitive again,*
> *The love-desperate banish'd knight*
> *With a fire in his brain*
> *Flying o'er the stormy main.* (lines 185-88)

After Tristram has married the second Iseult, Arnold follows la Villemarqué: "Toutefois c'est en vain qu'il essaie d'oublier son premier amour, c'est en vain qu'il court les aventures périlleuses; au lieu d'une distraction, il y trouve une blessure mortelle." But he expands this with the aid of his own imagination and with considerable help from Malory.

[the "boire d'amour"] et le partagea avec son amante, et en souffrit mainte douleur."

He describes Tristram's condition when Iseult first finds him and nurses him back to health. He refers to Tristram as "Launcelot's guest at Joyous Gard"; which is from Malory (X, lii), but Arnold omits to say that Iseult had been with him there. He has Tristram recall his fighting against "the chivalry of Rome": which would come from Malory's Book V *passim,* and is Arnold's simple transfer of the association of Tristram with Arthur's battles to the particular period of Tristram's marriage in Brittany. Just following this is a more interesting transfer: the narrator recalls Tristram's part in the conversion of the Rhineland—

> *And label with the blessed sign*
> *The heathen Saxons on the Rhine.*

This is of course an invention of Arnold's made up apparently by the conflation of two sections of Malory. In Book V, chap. viii, Arthur on his way to Rome "sent his people to Sessoine and took up the towns and castles from the Romans." This Sessoins (variously spelled) is conjectured to be Soissons. But in Book X, which is Malory's 'Second Book of Sir Tristram,' chap. xxviii, there is an account of Tristram's coming to the rescue of Mark when Cornwall was attacked by the Sessoins, i.e., the Saxons of southern England.[9]

In Part II, the last meeting and death of Tristram and Iseult of Ireland, Arnold plotted his own course. According to la Villemarqué Tristan sends for his first love to heal him, but his wife "qui a surpris le secret des amours de son mari, lui fait accroire que la reine de Cornouailles refuse de se rendre à ses vœux, et Tristan meurt de chagrin." Malory's account of Tristram's death belongs to a quite different tradition. In Book XIX, chap. xi, Mark "that traitor king slew the noble

[9] Malory is as usual a bit confused or vague. If Arnold had read Dunlop for this detail he would not easily have placed the Saxons on the Rhine (Dunlop, p. 86).

knight Sir Tristram, as he sat harping afore his lady La Beale
Isoud, . . . and La Beale Isoud died swooning upon the corse
of Sir Tristram, whereof was great pity." Only one detail
from Malory appears in Part II, the explanation of Tristram's
name. His mother, just before Tristram was born, "had taken
such cold for a default of help that deep draughts of death
took her, that she needs must die . . ." and she charged her
gentlewoman that the child should be called "Tristram, that
is as much as to say a sorrowful birth." Arnold here (II, 84)
quotes Malory direct.

Neither la Villemarqué nor Malory includes the picturesque
element of the black and white sails: and we have Arnold's
statement that he did not know about it: "a beautiful way of
ending," he wrote to Swinburne, "which I should perhaps
have used, had I known of it, but I did not." That is to say,
he did not know of it when he composed his poem, though he
must have met it later when he consulted Dunlop for his Note,
for Dunlop devotes nearly a page (p. 87) to it. And even if
he had wanted to use it he would have found considerable
difficulty in fitting it in with his version.

For this final scene of the *Liebestod,* however, Arnold may
have taken suggestions from his two sources. La Villemarqué
(p. 282) describes an Armorican "ballade" in which Yseult
has heard that Tristan is dead; she runs through the streets in
great despair; and the Bretons, who had never seen anyone so
beautiful, ask who she is. When she finds Tristan she cries:
"Beloved Tristan, when I see you dead I can no longer live;
you have died for love of me, I also will die of love, since I
could not come in time." Then she lies down beside him,
takes him in her arms, and gives up the ghost. And in Malory,
Book IX, chap. xx, there is a similar incident. Sir Andrew
has maliciously caused a report of Tristram's death to be circu-
lated. "But when Queen Isoud heard of these tidings she made

such sorrow that she was nigh out of her mind; and so upon a day she thought to slay herself and never live after Sir Tristram's death." But as she is about to fall on a sword Mark finds her and claps her into a tower.

There is one almost certain borrowing from Dunlop, the only one, it seems to me, which can be clearly recognized as such. The first two lines of Part III read in 1852:

> *A year had flown, and in the chapel old*
> *Lay Tristram and Queen Iseult dead and cold.*[10]

But in 1853, in the second edition, when Arnold added on Froude's suggestion his Note summarizing the whole story from "Dunlop's Hist. of fiction," these lines were altered to

> *A year had flown and o'er the sea away,*
> *In Cornwall, Tristram and Queen Iseult lay,*

and two were added:

> *At Tyntagil, in King Marc's chapel old:*
> *There in a ship they bore those lovers cold.*[11]

Malory says nothing of the burial of the lovers. For his first version Arnold may have taken a hint from la Villemarqué: "On trouve effectivement près de Tintagel, dans la Cournouaille anglaise, au bord de la mer, un rocher désigné sous le nom breton de *Lam Tristan,* ou Saut de Tristan" (p. 280). Dunlop (p. 87) reads:

Tristan, before his death, had requested that his body should be sent to Cornwall, and that his sword, with a letter he had written, should be delivered to King Marc. The remains of Tristan and Yseult were embarked in a vessel, along with the sword, which

[10] These two, preceded by lines 34-37, are written along the margin of the Yale manuscript (Tinker and Lowry, p. 121).

[11] So also in 1854; but in 1857, after Arnold had learned the correct accentuation of *Tyntagil,* they (along with several other lines in Part I) had to be revised.

was presented to the king of Cornwall. He was melted with tenderness when he saw the weapon which slew Morhoult of Ireland, which so often saved his life, and redeemed the honour of his kingdom. In the letter Tristan begged the pardon of his uncle, and related the story of the amorous potion.

Marc ordered the lovers to be buried in his own chapel.

Thus for his revision of 1853, when he had apparently for the first time consulted Dunlop, Arnold incorporated this one detail. Any other changes which may have occurred to him now—using the black and white sails, for example—he rejected, but this one, requiring the addition of only two lines, he adopted.

iii

"The story of Merlin," Arnold wrote to Clough, "is imported from the Morte d'Arthur." Actually he took from Malory's account of Merlin and Nimue, the damsel of the lake, (Book IV, chap. i) only the last line and the idea it represents:

For she was passing weary of his love.

Malory represents Merlin as assotted upon Nimue: "And always Merlin lay about the lady to have her maidenhood, and she was passing weary of him." Arnold's real sources for this story were la Villemarqué's article, "Visite au tombeau de Merlin," and Louandre's "L'Enchanteur Merlin." It would appear that he had access (at Thun?) to a series of issues of the *Revue de Paris,* bound or unbound, and that having become interested by la Villemarqué's article, "Les poèmes gallois," which gave him the Tristram story, he looked further and turned up these other two, one of the year 1837, the other of 1840. In fact, on the second page of "Les poèmes gallois" la Villemarqué remarks on Milton's early plans for an epic on the Arthurian cycle and adds: "Enfin il trouvait un pendant à souhait, en grace chaste et demi voilée, aux amours de son paradis dans l'histoire . . . de Merlin lui-même et de la fée Viviane." Perhaps this should be remembered as not only a hint leading to Arnold's use of Merlin and Vivian at the conclusion of his poem, but also as a hint accounting for Arnold's conception of the story.

The opening verses of Part III may owe something to la Villemarqué. Arnold describes the place where Iseult took her children to play as "a green circular hollow" with "till'd fields" and as a "cirque" surrounded by heather (which however "grows not here"). La Villemarqué describes the scene of Merlin's tomb as "un immense amphithéâtre," with "de champs remplis de blés ou de genets aux fleurs jaunes." Arnold later names primroses, without calling them yellow. There is nothing of this in Louandre: but it is from Louandre that Arnold gets the spelling *Broce-liande,* for which la Villemarqué has *Brécilien.* Both give much the same story, though from different French sources. Louandre takes a darker view of Merlin's amours, somewhat like Malory's and an even darker view of the Tristram and Iseult story: "un enchaînement d'adultères effrontés." Merlin meets in a forest a noble lady of brilliant complexion and chaste appearance; he addresses her with flattery, impresses her by contriving a magic park filled with knights and ladies at their pleasure, and obtains from her the promise to meet him in the same place a few months later. He is completely captivated, tells her all his secrets. One day when they are together in Brocéliande "il se reposa au pied d'un buisson d'aubépine et s'endormit. Viviane, qui épiait son sommeil, se leva doucement, détacha sa ceinture et, traçant avec cette ceinture un cerne autour de son amant, elle l'enferma pour toujours dans une enceinte sans issue." Why have you thus deceived me? cries Merlin. She, having used the formula without realizing its power, weeps, for she only wanted to keep him as her lover; but he is held in a "tour indestructible" "jusq'à la fin des siècles." Gawain, sent by Arthur, finds the tower and hears a voice coming forth from it: "Henceforth I can speak only with Vivian." It is said that Vivian still watches over him like a pious matron.

La Villemarqué's version is similar but he is more severe with Vivian. "Quand Viviane l'entend, par grande trahison, et pour le mieux décevoir, elle lui met les bras au cou, et le commence à baiser en disant qu'il peut bien être sien, puisqu'elle est sienne. . . . je veux que nous fassions un beau lieu par art et par engin, tel qu'il ne puisse jamais être défait, et vous et moi serons là, en joie et plaisir." Then follows the passage, already quoted by Tinker and Lowry, showing the closeness of Arnold's version to la Villemarqué's. Arnold rejected, however, the conclusion of the story in both his French sources; la Villemarqué's like Louandre's represents Vivian as regretting what she has done and wishing she could release Merlin. For his ending he turned to Malory. This might partially account for Arnold's statement that he imported the whole story from Malory; but it still leaves one puzzled why Arnold rejected the French ending. Perhaps the simplest explanation is that Malory provided him with a good last line.

"The story of Merlin, of which I am particularly fond, was brought in on purpose to relieve the poem which would else I thought have ended too sadly, but perhaps the new element introduced is too much." Thus Arnold to Hill, in the letter already quoted from, obviously in answer to criticism. Is the answer satisfying? Is the story a fitting one for Iseult to tell her little children? Does it relieve the sadness of the whole poem, and is it "too much"? This is not the only place in which Arnold set new and disconcerting matter at the end of a poem. One example is his 'Stanzas from the Grande Chartreuse': the children reared in the shade of the abbey which is and is not the Carthusian monastery. Another is the famous

simile at the end of 'The Scholar-Gipsy.' In all three a fresh
picture is added which tends to blur the main picture, and in
each case one may suspect Arnold of merely wishing to end
with a flourish; as he so eminently succeeded in doing, without
irrelevance, with the celebrated Oxus ending of 'Sohrab and
Rustum.' Whether the others are "too much" or not must be
left as a matter of taste.

The other two questions are closely related. We may take
Arnold's word for the story as diverting if not altogether cheerful; and we must be on guard against reading his version in the
light of Tennyson's, based on Malory and representing Vivian
as the wicked enchantress and Merlin as the besotted old man.[12]
We should rather read it in the light of Arnold's own text and
of what he made of the versions of la Villemarqué and Louandre; that is, a fairy-tale—how Vivian worked an enchantment
on Merlin because she was tired of him. Such a story, adorned
with much descriptive detail but divested of its sinister elements, might very well amuse the little children. Many
another story told to the little ones, Arnold might argue, would
be shocking if they understood its real implications. But is
there something deeper, either a bit of autobiography or an
obscure release for Iseult herself? Arnold's Vivian is given
blue eyes and she imprisons her lover in a "daisied circle."
Hence, it has been said, Arnold had in mind his own experience
with that "inviolable shade," Marguerite! And in truth there
are critics who find in all of 'Tristram and Iseult' mysterious
echoes of that Swiss love affair. On the other hand, if a par-

[12] Tennyson's first Vivien idyll was privately printed in *Enid and
Nimuë; The True and the False*, 1857. It was first published as one
of *Four Idylls of the King*, 1859, with its title changed from 'Nimuë' to
'Vivien.' The statement in the *Commentary*, p. 123, is inaccurate. On
the same page, n. 12, "L'Enchanteur Merlin" is wrongly attributed to
la Villemarqué, following a slip by Mrs. Sells; and it was Lowry who
first made the suggestion.

ticular significance is to be sought either in Arnold's selection
of the Merlin story here or in Iseult's choice of it to entertain
her children, it would have to be that Iseult is now cured of her
old love for Tristram and is reconciled to the domestic quiet
of her widowhood. She, like Vivian, had fallen under the
spell of passion, but all that is over and she is free. Or, like
Merlin, she had been a victim of enchantment and she is now
at peace. Or, reaching further back, her Tristram had suffered
under the love-spell of his Irish Iseult and is now released for
ever. But these are vain and gratuitous speculations. They
run counter to Arnold's own statement and they are not very
convincing if regarded as revelations from the dark deeps of
Arnold's unconscious mind.

iv

From this discussion of sources it is possible to come fairly
close to an understanding of what Arnold meant by "in the
main formed." His perusal of la Villemarqué's précis gave
him a simple triangular love story, with a medieval setting,
and this view he made quite clear in his insertion of ll. 56-82
of Part I for the second edition:

> *There were two Iseults who did sway*
> *Each her hour of Tristram's day . . .*

and so on: one possessed his "resplendent prime," the other his
"waning time." What attracted Arnold was the latter. We
may feel surprise at this, but we must take it as a fact. So he
began his poem with the latter, shrewdly choosing Tristram's
delirium for the purpose of 'flashbacks' to present the resplendent prime and thus subordinate what is for us the main
story but for him was background. This was excellent strategy,
though the plan miscarried, partly because of the difficulty in
making the antecedent action clear to his readers, and partly

because of the difficulty of making Tristram's marriage and the desolation of his widow sufficiently attractive in comparison. To keep Iseult of the White Hands in the foreground he introduces her first and elaborately emphasizes the pathos of her position. He dresses her in silk, gives her golden ringlets but "sunk and pale" cheeks, and describes her as a lonely orphan, a "sweet flower": "The sweetest Christian soul alive" with a "fragile loveliness." We cannot possibly miss the intention. More pathos is added by showing Tristram as a "fever-wasted wight" at the close of his resplendent life and as now in some sense a victim both of the magic draught and of the "proud . . . petulant . . . imperious" Irish Iseult. Part II presented a new problem, which Arnold solved neither to his nor to our satisfaction. When the Queen finally comes Tristram is at first harsh and almost truculent with her (but remember he is ill and dying); then he relents and Iseult defends herself. "Royal state" with her "deep-wrong'd husband" (this is a bow to the proprieties) has not changed her devotion, and she is now only "a faded watcher" and "humbled"; his "younger Iseult" need not fear her "former rival," in fact she will wish the Queen to remain always beside her (the conflicting loves reconciled). And Tristram dies with words of praise for his wife: "she [also] is of royal blood! . . . she is kind and good" (the Vere de Vere motif). Here similarly we cannot miss the intention. Arnold never looked more mid-nineteenth-century than here. And when he calls Iseult "Our snowdrop by the Atlantic sea" and brings on the two sleeping children—"Ah, tired madcaps!" and later "the feather'd hats of the sweet pair" —surely the cup runneth over.

All which of course but reveals Arnold's conception of the story he took from la Villemarqué. It was this which he "formed" on the Continent and found himself unwilling to alter when he read Malory and saw what the story really meant. The conception he could not change, but the amount of detail which he took from Malory (as shown above) almost proves that he had written nothing or very little before he returned to England.

A natural question, why Arnold gave just this interpretation to the story he read in the French article can only be answered conjecturally. One thinks of the emotional climate (as the fashionable term goes) of Arnold in 1848 or 1849, when he was breaking with Marguerite and not yet in love with Miss Wightman; but one discovers very little help here. By the time the poem was finished and published, 1852, things were different: he could have seen himself as a kind of Tristram at the apex of a love triangle, with Marguerite as a kind of Irish Iseult and Mrs. Arnold as Iseult of the White Hands. Thus it might even be that he took a deliberately antiromantic view of the whole story and meant to show the triangle resolved into domesticity. The Romantics had dealt with passion for passion's sake; by playing this down he would minimize the illicit love (Marguerite?) and enlarge on the beauty of domestic serenity, adding the children as prophetic of his own. Anyway, we may accept his interpretation of the old tale as a datum and consider the care with which he worked it up. On this score he merits no little praise. Given the handicaps of his method and his conception of the story, he has managed surprisingly well.[13] The fine poetical passages speak for themselves. One might say the same for the blemishes—though I have known readers who thought Part II the best. The Breton bard sinks more than once to bathos:

[13] That he was impenitent of failure is clear from his judgment on *Tristan und Isolde*, which he *saw* in March 1886: "I may say that I have managed the story better than Wagner. The second act is interminable, and without any action." After that he "was quite worn out and came away." The music did not interest him.—*Letters*, II, 374.

> *What new change shall we now see?*
> *A happier? Worse it cannot be.*

And such sub-Wordsworthian lines as

> *Sparkled with mocking glee and exercise. . . .*
> *For they had travell'd far and not stopp'd yet*

call for no comment. The criticism-of-life passage in Part III, withdrawn from two editions and then restored, is more noisy than impressive, besides being out of place. The numerous alterations in the closing scene of Part II—the "stately Huntsman" on the arras—hardly improve the aim for a spectacular finish.

v

Appreciation is not the immediate concern. I have tried by an examination of the evidence to remove some of the errors of previous studies of the poem and to show something of Arnold's intention in composing the kind of poem he chose to write. His curiously inadequate and even inaccurate statements about his sources are entirely characteristic. They have to be taken for what they are worth. They point a direction, no more. He read the story at Thun, he "had never met with it before, and it fastened upon" him. He decided at once to use it for a poem and sketched out a plan for his handling of it: "the poem was in the main formed." But he needed more material and when he "got back to England [he] looked at the Morte d'Arthur and took what [he] could." He must have looked at Malory with some care, for he not only took a great deal from Books VIII-IX and Book XII, which Malory calls the First and Second Books of Sir Tristram, but also from scattered places elsewhere. Malory of course provided an embarrassment of material which he had to reduce drastically in accord with his subordination of Tristram's early life and to transpose to fit his emphasis on Tristram's life in Brittany, and all the while adapt to his original scheme already formed "in the main" from la Villemarqué's article. Moreover, if the Merlin story was part of the original plan and not an "afterthought," he must have taken a hint from la Villemarqué and turned to other, earlier and later, volumes of the *Revue de Paris* for help. His words, "brought in on purpose to relieve" the sadness of the ending—Iseult alone on the Breton coast with her two children—are ambiguous on this point. But his other statement that Merlin was "imported from the Morte d'Arthur" would mean that it was no part of his original plan, but added, for the alleged reason, after he had returned to England. *Or* it might mean simply that he was already familiar with it—"of which I am particularly fond"—from Malory before he had met with the Tristram story, and hence associated with earlier memories of Malory. This would explain his use of the striking phrase at the end of Malory's chapter (IV, i) for his own last line, and suggest why he borrowed only that part of the Merlin story from Malory. But just as he had supplemented the French article with Malory in England, he supplemented his recollection of the Malory Merlin with the *other* French articles, either at Thun or later in England. Again his statements are ambiguous and, if not taken cautiously, may be misleading.

Finally, the special circumstances of Arnold's accumulation of material and the irregular development of his attitude towards the material throw some light on the poem itself and perhaps add some extenuation of Arnold's whole management of the story. If Arnold had at the outset informed himself fully concerning the substance and meaning of the action and characters he would, on his own admission, have written a different poem. But he committed himself, or thought he did, in advance, with insufficient knowledge, and the result is a kind of patchwork, all too obvious to the reader and a source of dissatisfaction to the author. Whether he could even so have mastered the handicaps of his chosen plan—the mingling of dramatic and lyrical forms, the dot-and-dash method of narration, with the emphasis on Tristram's decline and on the sufferings of his widow—is still another question. "The fusion of lyric with dramatic form," said Swinburne, "gives the highest type of poetry." Perhaps so, if one is thinking of Aeschylus or, *caeteris paribus, Atalanta in Calydon*. But Arnold tried the fusion in 'Empedocles on Etna' and in 'Tristram and Iseult,' without complete success. He was slow in learning that the dramatic technique was beyond his powers. He seems not to have grasped the problem of dramatic structure or to have possessed the depth of passion to conceive a "great action." His explanatory Preface in 1853 shows him thoroughly confused about the problem of 'Empedocles'; for while seeming to defend a Greek subject he allowed himself to imply a comparison with the best Greek tragedy. He "intended to delineate," he said, "the feelings of one of the last of the Greek religious philosophers"; and this he did with a considerable inweaving of his own "modern problems." That he produced a splendid psychological study of mental disintegration he hardly recognized and doubtless would have been unwilling to admit if convinced of it. He was probably also unreconciled to the fact that he produced in 'Tristram and Iseult' a sentimental version of a great tragic story, a version as Victorian as Tennyson's *Idylls* which were to follow, and equally without the powerful medieval background which is necessary to render the tragic story intelligible and moving.

5. *Arnold's Marguerite*[1]

THE 'PROBLEM' of Matthew Arnold's Marguerite is by way of becoming as much of a critical nuisance as that of Chaucer's Criseyde. In both there is no final judgment to be had, and it requires therefore a certain boldness to renew the quest (as in the present instance) without fresh and positive evidence. Something may be gained however from reviewing the 'case,' attempting to distinguish the known facts and the plausible deductions, and thus possibly clarifying the issue.

Marguerite is a problem, first, because so many rash and conflicting statements have been made about her, with a resultant confusion for anyone who might care to ascertain the truth. Yet it would be intolerably tedious, perhaps also presumptuous, to collect these statements and attempt controversially to confute or correct them, and I shall touch as lightly

[1] Reprinted with the kind permission of the University of North Carolina Press, from *Booker Memorial Studies,* edited by Hill Shine, Chapel Hill, [1950], pp. 78-103. The quotation from Mr. T. S. Eliot on p. 61 is from *The Use of Poetry and the Use of Criticism;* that from Stopford Brooke on p. 63 from his *Four Victorian Poets;* that from Professor Garrod on p. 83 from his *Poetry and the Criticism of Life;* and that from Sir E. K. Chambers from his Warton Lecture, 1932. The letter of Mr. Andrew S. Cairncross appeared in *T.L.S.* for 28 March 1935; the note by Mr. H. M. Walbrook in the London *Bookman* for May 1930, pp. 109-12. All the other references will be easily identified.

as possible on this part of the subject. But Marguerite is a really important problem in the biography of Arnold—to say nothing of the poetry she inspired, some very good and some less good—because she illuminates that conflict in Arnold's life and character which Professor E. K. Brown has recently studied from quite another point of view in his *Matthew Arnold, A Study in Conflict*. She has a poetical significance and a biographical significance both inescapable and both ramifying in various directions.

i

Readers of Arnold's second volume of verse, *Empedocles on Etna and Other Poems,* 1852 (they were certainly few), when they came to the series of eleven poems beginning on page 73 with 'The River' and ending with 'To Marguerite' may have noted fragments of a love story: first the distant and hopeless wooing, then the fevered meeting, followed by separation and resignation. And so, it seems reasonable to suppose, Arnold intended the series to be read. The lady's name was Marguerite, and there were sufficient circumstantial details to give the story an air of reality. If there were inconsistencies, they might pass unnoticed: certainly the details were hardly enough to warrant deducing a complete or coherent narrative. And if the incidents were drawn from two separate experiences, *that* would be an irrelevant matter. In point of fact, at least one reader, Mr. Andrew S. Cairncross, more than eighty years later (1935), saw fit to understand these poems as parts of "a single novelette in verse." The two women, he found, were "types, representing passion and ideal love—Marguerite and Urania. . . . The leading intention was to contrast the arch mockery and promiscuous passion of Marguerite—*la femme sensuelle moyenne*—with the disillusioned idealism of Urania, and the physical passion of the poet's own nature with his aspiration to spiritual love." And a few years before this, Mr. H. M. Walbrook had suggested that Arnold's Marguerite story was "a *donnée* worth considering" by some properly qualified contemporary in search of material for an idyllic romance. With these speculations I am not concerned, but they would perhaps have gratified Arnold.

When in the next year Arnold published under his full name *Poems. A New Edition* (a selection from his two preceding volumes together with eight new poems), the reader would have missed the first six of the series, the six expressing hopeless love for an inaccessible lady, and would have noted that four of the others, with two new ones, were grouped under the heading 'Switzerland.' In successive re-editions of his poems Arnold shifted the order and altered the content of this group, until in the *Selected Poems* of 1878 they stood as we now read them. But already in 1853, when the group was set up and the other poems withdrawn, it was clear that Arnold meant to limit the canon of Marguerite poems by the new title and that he did not intend the poems which had formerly preceded them to be read as parts of her 'story.' He might change the order of the 'Switzerland' poems, add to them, or take old ones away, but those which he placed in the 'Switzerland' group were manifestly the poems which he wished us to read as Marguerite's poems. (See Note on the Rearrangements of the Poems, pages 79 ff. below.)

In 1855, moreover, when he published *Poems. Second Series,* Arnold collected four of the eleven poems which in 1852 looked like a continuous series, and added one new one, under the heading 'Faded Leaves': and these were not reprinted until the Collected Edition of 1869, vol. 1. Yet in spite of this very marked separation of the two groups by Arnold himself and in spite of the noticeable differences in setting and in descriptive detail, readers and critics have persisted in confusing and even in confounding them; and likewise persisted in adding freely to the Marguerite canon on their own responsibility.

On the other hand, readers and critics of Arnold have been more cautious in assuming the reality of this Marguerite. "It is not easy to decide," said Saintsbury, for example, "and it is perhaps in both senses impertinent to speculate whether the Marguerite of the poems had any live original." Mr. T. S. Eliot has dismissed her as "at best a shadowy figure, neither very passionately desired nor very closely observed, a mere pretext for lamentation." But most of the others have accepted her as real on the evidence of the poems, though usually with some safeguarding phrase. Since the publication of Arnold's letters to Clough (edited by Dr. Lowry in 1932), however, the assumption is strengthened: for on 29 September 1848 Arnold wrote to Clough, from Leukerbad: "Tomorrow I repass the Gemmi and get to Thun, linger one day at the Hotel Bellevue for the sake of the blue eyes of one of its inmates: and then proceed by slow stages down the Rhine . . . to England." And from Thun, 23 September 1849, Arnold told Clough: "I wrote to you from this place last year," and in the same letter copied a portion of the Marguerite poem, 'A Parting,' which he was apparently then composing. In view of this evidence it is difficult to avoid the conclusion that Marguerite was a real person, even in the face of Arnold's reported denial; and such a conclusion, though it is of course based on inference, is further supported by two general considerations. Many of Arnold's poems are occasional in the sense that they took their origin in special circumstances, and the 'Switzerland' poems certainly seem to be of this sort: some of them are circumstantial to a degree hardly consistent with fictional invention. Moreover, if the 'Switzerland' poems had been intended as fiction Arnold might have been expected to make them less fragmentary and more coherent. One recalls, to be sure, his handling of the Tristram story, which is fragmentary enough, but Arnold was uncomfortable about his "management" of it; and there is no record of his dissatisfaction with the 'Switzerland' poems on this ground.

The conclusion then that Marguerite was a real person and that the experience reported in her poems represents a real experience may be regarded as justifiable, but the inferences to be drawn from it are another matter. No one will read the poems as a record which is factually accurate in all respects. But one may reconstruct the simple outlines somewhat as follows: Arnold met at Thun in 1848, or a year earlier, a young woman whom in the poems he calls Marguerite and enjoyed a mild flirtation with her—he had not yet settled down, it should be remembered, and begun snuffing after "a moral atmosphere." The next year he returned to Thun, still in love but now disturbed by that anxious choice which agitated his breast so intensely, the choice, phrased variously, between the world and the individual, between the demands of society and the urge to be himself; and this choice now took visible form in Marguerite. Should he give rein to his impulses or obey the God's tremendous voice, with which were perhaps mingled the paternal tones of Dr. Arnold's memory? So he lectures himself and her, finds himself wanting in passion and her in faith, feels exalted and cast down by turns; and then while he is crying Yea and sighing Nay, there appears a stranger with grey eyes which remind him of her blue eyes. This stranger is perhaps the *"unerreichbare schöne"* with whom Arnold fell in love, in the summer of 1850, and whom (after his appointment as inspector of schools had been arranged) he married in June 1851.

Mr. Walbrook asks a natural question: "Is it credible that if this story of enchantment, jealousy and anguish were one of actual fact, Matthew Arnold of all men would have gone pouring it forth to the public during the early years of his perfectly happy married life? Or that, under any circumstances, he would have committed a Marguerite whom he had not only loved and lost but also, in the bitterness of his disillusionment, harshly analyzed, to the stray speculations of any stranger picking up the book?" To this one can reply that other poets have frequently done much the same thing. There are, for example, Shakespeare in the Sonnets, Byron and Shelley *passim,* and doubtless many another if we possessed all the facts. Many a Victorian poet followed the same path, each in his different way—Rossetti and Patmore notably—but Arnold was never a complete Victorian in the cant sense of that adjective. He deplored the introspective habits of the great Romantics. There is, however, an inevitable conflict between the urge to create and the restraints of reticence, and probably each poet has thought of himself as keeping well on the right side of personal revelation. If a case is to be made out against Arnold it would be in connection with the 'Faded Leaves' poems, which, however innocuous on moral grounds, are on æsthetic grounds hardly as complimentary as one might wish; and since they add less than a cubit to Arnold's poetic stature one might question the taste of publishing them at all. Or, in other words, if Mrs. Arnold was to be sensitive about Marguerite, what would she think of herself in print, her poems alongside Marguerite's in 1852 and she herself apparently as a grey-eyed "stranger" in one of Marguerite's poems? (It is not impossible that there was even some interchange during the earliest stages of composition between the 'Switzerland' and the 'Faded Leaves' poems; and in 'The Buried Life' there are signs of two different women.) But the fatuity of all such divagations is reached in Stopford Brooke's comment on the "flowery track" stanza of 'The Terrace at Berne': "I do not think that the poet could ever have really loved the girl, else the memory of tenderness and of passion would have spared her that conjecture."

ii

About the young woman herself we know next to nothing
except a few details of her appearance and the fact that she was
French—and also the fact that she was not the one to determine Arnold's choice.   Her pale cheeks "of languid hue";
her "soft kerchief'd hair"; and particularly "those sweet eyes
of blue"; her "clear voice," "buoyant as morning"; and her
"arch smile"—these are a lover's description and tell us little.
It is something perhaps to hear of

> *The unconquer'd joy in which her spirit dwells*

and to learn that she had embraced other men before Arnold
met her and that when he returned to Switzerland she no
longer loved him; and also that years afterward he wondered
if she had become a Paris prostitute.   For the rest, we may take
our cue from one who knew her best, and not

> *try*
> *To things by mortal course that live*
> *A shadowy durability*
> *For which they are not meant, to give.*

The language is crabbed, but it is Arnold's last word about her,
his last farewell to her, and the phrase, for the sake of which
he gallantly sacrificed both rime and order, is almost a perfect
summary.   The woman who in 1848 had so moved his "starting, feverish heart," had achieved by 1863, after his marriage
and twelve years of school inspecting, after domestic love and
the *world* had made their way with him—the young woman
whom he called Marguerite had achieved only a *shadowy*
durability, a shadowy *durability*.

> *Go then!*

in one breath; and in the next—

> *Stay with me, Marguerite still!*

But it is not about Marguerite that we care to know, so much as about her poet. Of the nine poems which can certainly be called hers we cannot establish the dates of composition. We seem to see her first with an Olivia in 'A Dream.' This is a bit of almost humorously grandiloquent blank verse—

> *They saw us, they conferr'd; their bosoms heaved,*
> *And more than mortal impulse fill'd their eyes.*

Then he and his companion Martin are carried past by the "Loud thundering" river of life—which may well be a fanciful extension of the River Aar. The next poem, with its long title, 'To My Friends, Who Ridiculed a Tender Leave-Taking,' later reduced to 'A Memory Picture,' is overtly playful and Horatian: they may laugh, but

> *I, with little land to stir,*
> *Am the exacter labourer;*

and painting a detailed portrait of her lilac kerchief, soft face, arch chin, pale cheek, and so on, he cherishes the memory of a blithe flirtation. It has its place in the story, of course, but it is a frivolous little poem, what his family expected of him rather than the serious portions of the 1849 volume and was of course properly segregated to the Early Poems (in 1878).

The 'Switzerland' group begins with 'Meeting,' first called rather pointlessly 'The Lake' (*i.e.,* Thunersee). He sees Marguerite "again" (and now the printed page refers us by a note to 'A Memory Picture' of the preceding year), but as he springs to make his choice he is constrained by "a God's tremendous voice." The significant word is *choice*. Between the tender leave taking and this meeting he has been home and seen the necessity of settling down; now he escapes for a holiday in Switzerland looking for peace, putting ambition behind him, and to the voice and the "Powers who join and part" he answers:

Ah, warn some more ambitious heart,
And let the peaceful be!

'Parting' is a companion piece to 'Meeting,' but it is not so much a parting of lovers as a parting of the ways. He is making his choice between Marguerite and the mountains, between love, all for love, and the romantic solitude which is peace if not comfort. Here we begin to be on firm biographical ground. Writing to Clough 23 September 1849, Arnold says, "I wrote to you from this place [Thun] last year," and this letter seems to be lost, but that from Leukerbad, 29 September 1848, helps to fill in certain details. On Wednesday, 27 September, Arnold was at Domodossola immune to the attractions of the *"superbes filles"* seen there by his guide; on Thursday he crossed the Simplon on his way to Leukerbad, where he wrote Friday that he would "repass the Gemmi" the next day. And to *re*pass the Gemmi could only mean return to Thun. Evidently he had been in Thun earlier in the month. In this same letter he speaks disrespectfully of womankind and thus implies that he is already less than completely captivated by Marguerite. "I am glad to be tired of an author [Béranger]: one link in the immense series of cognoscenda and indagenda despatched. More particularly is this my feeling with regard to (I hate the word) women. We know beforehand all they can teach us: yet we are obliged to learn it directly from them."

The next summer (1849) he was again on the Continent and suggested to Clough a meeting at Geneva early in August. By 23 September he was in Thun once more—how much earlier we do not know—and from the tone of his long letter to Clough then he was evidently far from calm: ". . . these are damned times . . . light profligate friends, moral desperadoes like Carlyle, our own selves. . . ." The particular allusion to Marguerite is as follows: "I am here in a curious and not altogether comfortable state: however tomorrow I carry my aching head to the mountains and to my cousin the Blümlis Alp." And after quoting nine lines from 'Parting' he adds: "Yes, I come, but in three or four days I shall be back here, and then I must try how soon I can ferociously turn towards England."

At the same time Arnold was at work also on the first 'Obermann' poem, from which he copied out two lines, and he lamented that he had "never yet succeeded in any one great occasion in mastering" himself—"at the critical point I am too apt to hoist up the mainsail to the wind and let her drive"—but he hoped for improvement. Now the 'Stanzas in Memory of the Author of "Obermann"' were "conceived and partly composed," said Arnold in his note to the poem, "in the valley going down from the foot of the Gemmi Pass towards the Rhone"—that is, on the way to Leukerbad. The stanza referring to Wordsworth, he explained in a footnote, was written in November 1849. (Later he gave the whole poem the subtitle 'November 1849.') Our next date is from the letter to Clough written from Rugby in mid-November of this year. The evidence is not altogether satisfactory, but it seems to indicate that he lingered in Switzerland through October and it might be construed to mean that he fled to the Blümlis Alp more than once while he was making his choice.

In 'Parting' the mountains call him, and the voice of Marguerite, real or imagined, detains him. He cries to the mountains "I come"; he takes leave of Marguerite, telling her that their "different past" is a barrier between them and that their "spirits have grown" apart; and he beseeches Nature to calm and restore him. The letter and the poem agree perfectly. Then follows the poem 'A Farewell,' which does not contain her name and when first published, in 1852, was kept distinct from her other poems, and which, while its fits the chronology, contains some inconsistencies disturbing to the coherence of the story.

It is clear, however, that Arnold was at Thun twice in September 1848, with an interval in the mountains, and likewise twice in September-October 1849, with a similar interval in the mountains, at least as far as Leukerbad, escaping from himself and from Marguerite. As 'Parting' describes the desire to escape, so 'A Farewell' describes his return and final break with Marguerite. They embrace warmly and weep together, "with hearts too full to speak." He had in the preceding poem told himself, but obviously not her, that they were not suited for each other; and he tries again. "Days flew," he reports in the poem, while in terms of the letter he had already written to Clough he was trying ferociously to turn towards England. Days fly and Marguerite becomes cool. But he does not blame her, rather he deplores his own inconstancy and want of "trenchant force"—here one should read the canceled poem 'Destiny'—and he dismisses her, though not without a truculent note, with the prophecy that they will meet in a future life, all passion spent,

> *Ennobled by a vast regret,*
> *And by contrition seal'd thrice sure,*

and quench

> *The thirst for peace a raving world*
> *Would never let us satiate here.*

It is all somewhat Byronic, but it tells us plainly that he has learned not to trust his impulses and not to sacrifice his future for an unstable passion.

These details are, it should go without saying, not to be taken with biographical literalness. But they echo his letters, which in turn add corroborative verisimilitude to his account of Marguerite, and they (letters and poems together) show

something of the storm and stress which preceded his surrender
to the world only a little more than a year later.

The story ends as Arnold had foreseen. His decision made,
he turned towards England, reflecting that

> *we forget because we must*
> *And not because we will;*

that he is not exactly calmed and ennobled by his decision, but
only chilled by it; and crying—

> *Stay with me, Marguerite, still!*

But in this very poem, 'Absence,' he tells of meeting a "fair
stranger" with grey eyes who reminds him of Marguerite; and
whether by coincidence or by design these may well be the

> *Eyes too expressive to be blue,*
> *Too lovely to be grey,*

the grey eyes of the "stranger" of 'Faded Leaves,' that is to say,
of Miss Wightman. If this poem is of the autumn of 1849
and Arnold's courtship of his wife was in the summer of 1850
(which is what the books tell us), the overlapping is a felicitous
accident, a poetic rather than a biographic truth. Then ten
years pass (a round number) and in 1863 Arnold looks from
'The Terrace at Berne' across at his cousin the Blümlis Alp and
back to Marguerite. For she is "with him still"—"my Marguerite." He speculates rather harshly on what has become of
her; they have met and passed on the sea of life; and this is the
end, peace, so far as Marguerite is concerned.

Now we may return and follow the same path through
other poems. While Arnold was taking leave of Marguerite
and seeking calm in the mountains he found at first only
another unrest in the fevered pages of Obermann. In 'Parting'
he listened for "The mountain bee's hum" and in the Obermann stanzas—

> *Yet, through the hum of torrent lone,*
> *And brooding mountain-bee,*
> *There sobs I know not what ground-tone*
> *Of human agony.*

And here also he faced his choice:

> *Ah! two desires toss about*
> *The poet's feverish blood.*
> *One drives him to the world without,*
> *And one to solitude.*

Like the ideal poet in 'Resignation' (composed some while before) he believes that

> *He who hath watch'd, not shared, the strife,*
> *Knows how the day hath gone.*
> *He only lives with the world's life,*
> *Who hath renounced his own.*

So now, in November 1849, having given up Marguerite he gives up Senancourt (and in the 1852 volume 'A Farewell' immediately precedes the 'Stanzas')—

> *Away the dreams that but deceive,*
> *And thou, sad guide, adieu!*
> *I go, fate drives me; but I leave*
> *Half of my life with you. . . .*
>
> *I in the world must live*

leaving half of his life behind: an unhappy, unwilling choice, also with a poetical sequel. For the *New Poems* (1867) in which he first published 'The Terrace at Berne' closes with 'Obermann Once More,' still with "the wild bee's Alpine hum," though in another part of Switzerland. Here where Arnold for once associates himself with the great Victorian optimism, letting Obermann lament his "frustrate life" and celebrate prophetically the glories of Victorian prosperity, he proclaims himself **as**

> *serene,*
> *Yet tinged with infinite desire*
> *For all that might have been—*
>
> *The harmony from which man swerved*
> *Made his life's rule once more!*

The language is perhaps deliberately cryptic and subject to interpretation. It suggests however an imperfect reconciliation, resignation rather than content: the harmony which he had missed long ago and still yearns for. Serene, yes, like the later Matthew Arnold of the essays, and bland and slightly supercilious, but unsatisfied; the "Once-long'd-for storms of love" given over for quiet domestic love and family life, the solitude and contemplation sacrificed for the dusty world and a life of school inspecting, regret and still imperfect harmony for himself.

This conflict, which led to this issue, is bodied forth, moreover, in another poem of the 'Empedocles' volume—"Marguerite's book," as Professor Garrod perversely called it; for the inconstant Marguerite is certainly one element of his chaos, but certainly she does not dominate the volume. In 'A Summer Night' the moonlight charges him with hesitation between the active life and his own inner desires.

> *Hast thou then still the old unquiet breast,*
> *Which neither deadens into rest,*
> *Nor ever feels the fiery glow*
> *That whirls the spirit from itself away,*
> *But fluctuates to and fro,*
> *Never by passion quite possess'd*
> *And never quite benumb'd by the world's sway?*

This, it seems to me, sums up perfectly, almost epigrammatically, the mental turmoil of which Marguerite was a part; and at the end of the poem the "silent pain" of those

> *Who have long'd deeply once, and long'd in vain*

may be an allusion to her share of it—"long'd," notice, not "loved."

The cross-reference in Arnold's notes to 'A Southern Night,' written in 1859 or 1860, to 'A Summer Night' is more puzzling than helpful. The former poem says that the soft moonlight at Cette reminds him of a similar night "of yore" and a trouble now forgotten. The latter poem contains two moonlight pictures, the principal one of moonlight over the housetops of a deserted street, and a subordinate inset picture of a then "past night, and a far different scene," which corresponds fairly closely with the picture in 'A Southern Night.' Mr. Frederick Page has suggested that the reference is to the Marguerite poem 'A Farewell,' but this can hardly be so because the details of the inset picture (moonlit deep, spring tide, glistening bay) do not fit the Thunersee background at all; and the principal moonlight picture of 'A Summer Night' is so general that it would fit any setting with a street. In any case the figure of Marguerite is dim here.

Nor is she more than a background figure in that rather unexpected outburst in Part III of 'Tristram and Iseult'—the "gradual furnace of the world" in which our spirits are withered and our pleasures staled—

> *This, or some tyrannous single thought, some fit*
> *Of passion, which subdues our souls to it, . . .*
> *Call it ambition, or remorse, or love.*

Nor does the intrusive image of Vivian at the end resemble Marguerite save for her blue eyes and what she has in common with the universal *femme fatale*. Vivian's seduction of Merlin and Marguerite's spell over her poet are poles asunder.

Two poems of the 'Switzerland' group remain to be considered: they are hardly parts of the story, yet significant elements of the picture. The other poems of the group are but small stars in Arnold's poetic diadem; the 'Isolation' poems, in spite of their handicap of shifting and unfortunate titles, are Marguerite's triumph, her immortality, the tokens of her durability. The first, as we now read them, though not published till five years after the other, is perhaps artistically less successful, with its juxtaposition of modern rhetoric—

> *The fault was grave! . . .*
> *Thou lov'st no more;—Farewell! Farewell!*
>
> *Farewell!—and thou, thou lonely heart . . .*
> *Back to thy solitude again!*

and the classical picture of Luna and Endymion, and the homiletic note of

> *to prove*
> *This truth—to prove and make thine own;*

but the conclusion is near Arnold's lyric best:

> *Or, if not quite alone, yet they*
> *Which touch thee are unmating things—*
> *Ocean and clouds and night and day;*
> *Lorn autumns and triumphant springs;*
> *And life, and others' joy and pain,*
> *And love, if love, of happier men.*
>
> *Of happier men—for they, at least,*
> *Have* dream'd *two human hearts might blend*
> *In one, and were through faith released*
> *From isolation without end*
> *Prolong'd; nor knew, although not less*
> *Alone than thou, their loneliness.*

The other,

> *Yes! in the sea of life enisled . . .*
> *The unplumb'd, salt, estranging sea*

is Arnold's lyric best, though marred by one or two infelicities.

It is or should be revealing that when the "winds of passionate welcome and farewell" are blown away, the poetic theme of Marguerite's love is isolation—not, as one critic has phrased it, "the spiritual isolation which must ever separate two souls who are respectively involved; the woman in the gay, romantic life of Paris and of Switzerland, the man in the austere service of Faith," but rather the annihilating sense of isolation which overwhelms two lovers (or one of them) at the failure of love, when "their longing's fire" is "as soon as kindled, cool'd" and there is no blending of their hearts or spirits. This is Arnold's secret, if we are to put any trust in his poetic sincerity. In 'Destiny' he asked why with

> *A heart of ice, a soul of fire*

he was always striving

> *To love more deeply than he can.*

Now he recognizes that Marguerite has not been able to arouse in him such a passion as he would like to feel, that the whole affair is a failure because neither of them was sufficiently moved. In other Marguerite poems he makes his excuses: she was not this, he was not that. But apparently the truth is that he wanted to fall passionately in love, but never quite succeeded because she did not really melt his heart of ice. Afterward, to be sure, as well as during the stress and strain, he cherished the experience since it was the one experience in which he nearly was swept away, as a young man and admirer of Byron would wish to be; which had taught him perhaps that such love was not for him. It was failure on both sides, and its sharpest pressure was that sense of isolation, of the predestined and insuperable barrier between souls which have eagerly desired to unite and could not.

The double irony of the sequel is another matter. For he

had no sooner dismissed Marguerite and forsaken Obermann, he had no sooner admitted to himself that love is not enough and that he must accept the world, than he became equally eager to win Miss Wightman, and, that accomplished, he heard the Justice's "tremendous voice" speaking for the world and financial security: a very practical criticism of life. Or in the words of Sir Edmund Chambers:

Certainly the parting with a blue-eyed girl became for Matthew Arnold something more than itself, a parting with the whole world of passionate romance which he put behind him. The Marguerite poems are not merely poems of isolation, but of renunciation, of self-dedication. There had been a κάθαρσις. He turned back to his 'sphered course', to the rigorous teachers who had seized his youth, . . . and incidentally to the routine, which he often found irksome, of the Education Office.

There is some exaggeration in this, and some truth. The Education Office was more than an incident. Marguerite is more than the symbol, less than the whole, of Arnold's conflict when the 'worldling' was rapidly maturing into the 'prophet.' The real note of the Marguerite poems is that of unrealized passion, self-thwarted: a private revelation, a renunciation, and a kind of catharsis. But it was Justice Wightman (so one reads the evidence) who *ab extra* assigned him the lesser rôle of Martha and propelled the poet into a career of self-dedication to culture and, to use the modern word, service.

But after the die was cast it was still difficult to forget. In January 1851, the year of his marriage, Arnold wrote to his sister K: "The aimless and unsettled, but also open and liberal state of our youth we *must* perhaps all leave and take refuge in our morality and character; but with most of us it is a melancholy passage from which we emerge shorn of so many beams that we are almost tempted to quarrel with the law of nature which imposes it on us." In 1853, already tired of inspecting schools and longing for the restfulness of a diplomatic post, he wrote to his wife: "All this afternoon I have been haunted by a vision of living with you at Berne, on a diplomatic appointment." And the next year: "How I should like to live quietly in Switzerland with you and the boys." And in March 1856 to his brother William: "I on the contrary half cannot half will not throw myself into it [his work] and feel the weight of it doubly in consequence. I am inclined to think it would have been the same with any active line of life on which I had found myself engaged." And in May 1857 to his sister: "I have a positive thirst to see the Alps again, and two or three things I have in mind which I cannot finish till I have again breathed and smelt Swiss air." Two of these we have just seen, 'The Terrace at Berne' and 'Obermann Once More.' One does not suppose that he brooded over Marguerite, or that on the other hand he kept the memory of her as a literary convenience. He still felt the retroaction of his crisis of 1849, still had to "slip his chain," and still thought of "all that *might* have been," and could not deny himself a longing backward look—as Orpheus to Marguerite's Eurydice.

iii

There is certainly no need to exaggerate the claims of Marguerite on posterity. Her two principal poems and several lines and phrases from others constitute her immortality, and they are perhaps more than as a person she deserves. *Sic se res habent.* But her importance to Arnold is another matter and requires careful summary. Setting aside the two lighter pieces which Arnold finally removed to Early Poems, her seven poems present an almost plotted sequence: the troubled meeting in 1849, the trial parting in search of peace, the harsh farewell, the lyric interlude on a theme of isolation, and the oddly named 'Absence' which confesses his unwilling renunciation—and also, perhaps, serves as transition to another love which ended in marriage. And then the long coda wherein Arnold explains that he is done with her, ten years after. Now, however much he may have dramatized himself and her, the note of actuality, the amount of circumstantial detail, and the air of verisimilitude are unmistakable, are in fact clearer than in 'Faded Leaves,' which is known to be biographical. We can hardly err therefore in giving them general, although not literal, credence. Or if the family tradition, as represented by his daughter Lady Sandhurst, is to be accepted: "that Arnold always insisted 'Marguerite' was imaginary," she was a work of the creative imagination which is often truer than bare truth. Yet it is hard to believe that the verses which too often have an air of impromptu, of spontaneous overflow, or outburst, of immediate feeling, and are some of them so rough as to betray the disorder of untranquil emotion—the two isolation poems always excepted—sprang from imagination alone. Nowhere else did Arnold show that kind of imagination. But what could he say, if pressed directly? or in what tone, with what inflection, did he say "imaginary"? Useless questions, for however the elementary details were embroidered for poetical ends, there was a Marguerite with whom he rehearsed a part and from whom he learned that it was no part for him to play.

Arnold might have said of 'Switzerland' what Meredith said of 'Modern Love': "A writer's verse is one of his methods of relieving himself of the burden within him"; and he might have quoted—

We are betrayed by what is false within.

There are those who set a high value on passionate feeling and its transcendent power to exalt and even ennoble; there are those who envy the few who are capable of this intense emotion and unselfish absorption, for in its denial of the world and social

obligations it has some kinship with religious ecstasy; but there
are also those who set a higher value on their moral integrity
and the strength of will and intellect, who cannot bear to
surrender this integrity to the mere feelings, who (having
learned from the moth) desire the flame only provided it is
hard and gemlike and so are neither for Jehovah nor for his
enemies. Arnold was one of these last. At his youthful crisis,
which came rather late—for he was, at twenty-seven, still the
'worldling,' at least in the eyes of his family, and he had settled
down only to the extent of becoming secretary to Lord Lans-
downe two years before—he was perplexed by the choice between the world and solitude. In the sonnet he praised Shakespeare's aloofness from mortal affairs; in 'Resignation' he ex-
tolled the ideal poet's detachment from mundane entangle-
ments; his Empedocles plunged into the crater because in
freeing himself from the world he could not escape from
"thought," could not live in the light of his own soul—the
dilemma from both sides; his Mycerinus withdrew in scorn
from the world and its unjust gods to "the silence of the groves"
and "the tumult of the feast"—and again Arnold betrayed his
uncertainty by hinting that the king held aloof from the revelry
and so

Was calm'd, ennobled, comforted, sustain'd.

What course was *he* to choose? Poetry, the life contemplative,
in the light of his own soul, in peace, away from "the raving
world"? or that very world,

the ungenial earth,
Man's work-place,

with its promises and satisfactions? Well, he separated himself,
as he put it, from Obermann (solitude and contemplation)
and he renounced Marguerite (poetry and passion) at the same
time. They had for him the reality of symbols; and it was

Marguerite's rôle and opportunity to teach him—"We know beforehand all they can teach us: yet we are obliged to learn it directly from them"—that the heroic quality which holds the world well lost was not his. Perhaps she was right, whatever else. But he was never quite convinced. One should ponder his words in a letter to Clough as early as 1 May 1853: "I feel immensely—and more clearly—what I have (I believe) lost and choked by my treatment of myself"; and one should read in the light of these words both 'The Terrace at Berne' and 'Obermann Once More,' and that strange *poème de noces* 'Stanzas from the Grande Chartreuse,' together with many other phrasings in verse and prose: his dissatisfaction with the choice. When he writes

And Marguerite I shall see no more

and brings Obermann on preaching Victorian progress, it is not so much that he mourns her loss or denies Senancourt's philosophy, as that he mourns his own loss and would return to Senancourt's solitude, slipping his chain. Perhaps the choice was right, for him; but he was still unreconciled. What we mourn, however, is that in the test of character (that modern shibboleth) Marguerite was not the woman to save him for poetry, and to save him from a life of school inspecting and journalistic controversies.

NOTE ON THE REARRANGEMENTS OF THE POEMS

In the 1849 volume, *The Strayed Reveller and Other Poems, By A.,* only one of the Marguerite poems appeared: 'To My Friends, Who Ridiculed a Tender Leave-Taking,' later renamed 'A Memory Picture.'

The next volume, *Empedocles on Etna, and Other Poems,* 1852, contained, after the title poem:

'The River'	(in 1855 'Faded Leaves i')
'Excuse'	(in 1869 'Urania')

'Indifference'	(in 1869 'Euphrosyne')
'Too Late'	(in 1855 'Faded Leaves ii')
'On the Rhine'	(in 1855 'Faded Leaves iv')
'Longing'	(in 1855 'Faded Leaves v')
'The Lake'	(in 1853 'Switzerland ii')
'Parting'	(in 1853 'Switzerland iv')
'Absence'	(in 1853 'Switzerland vi')
'Destiny'	(not reprinted by Arnold)
'To Marguerite'	(in 1853 'Switzerland v')
['Yes, in the sea']	

After ten more titles, including 'Tristram and Iseult,' appeared 'A Farewell,' which in 1854 became 'Switzerland v.' This early arrangement of some 'Faded Leaves' poems and some 'Switzerland' poems consecutively is to be noted.

In the next year, 1853, Arnold published, under his full name, *Poems. A New Edition* (later called *Poems. First Series*); it was a selection from the two preceding volumes, with eight new poems. Here the 'Switzerland' group was first set up:

> i. 'To My Friends'
> ii. 'The Lake'
> iii. 'A Dream'
> iv. 'Parting'
> v. 'To Marguerite'
> vi. 'Absence'

The poems which here precede and follow are unrelated to either the 'Switzerland' or the 'Faded Leaves' group. There were no 'Faded Leaves' poems in this volume. In 1854 a new edition was issued, containing of course no 'Faded Leaves' poems, but with one change in the 'Switzerland' group, namely 'A Farewell' (which was not in the 1853 volume) was brought from its previous isolated position in the 1852 volume and became 'Switzerland v'—the v and vi of 1853 now becoming vi and vii.

In the following year, 1855, appeared *Poems. Second Series,* a selection from the volumes of 1849 and 1852, but reprinting nothing from the 1853 and 1854 volumes. Here first the 'Faded Leaves' group was set up:

      i. 'The River'
     ii. 'Too Late'
    iii. 'Separation'
    iv. 'On the Rhine'
     v. 'Longing'

These were followed by 'Self-Deception,' then 'Excuse' and 'Indifference' (which in 1852 had stood between 'The River' and 'Too
Late' as though they belonged together) and 'Resignation,' etc.

    Two years later, in 1857, appeared the Third Edition of the
1853 volume. It also of course contained no 'Faded Leaves' poems;
but it added one new 'Switzerland' poem, "We were apart. . ."
entitled 'To Marguerite.'

    Arnold's next volume of poems (except *Merope,* 1858) came ten
years later: *New Poems,* 1867. It contained two new poems of
interest here, 'Calais Sands' and 'The Terrace at Berne. 'Dover
Beach,' which was also new, stood just between. In 1868 there was
a second edition of this volume.

    In 1869 appeared the so-called First Collected Edition, volume i
of which contained the 'Faded Leaves' group from 1855, and volume
ii the 'Switzerland' group, as in 1857 (except for the omission of 'A
Dream'), followed immediately by 'Urania' (which had previously
been called 'Excuse'), 'Euphrosyne' (which had previously been
called 'Indifference'), 'Calais Sands,' 'Dover Beach,' etc. Here it is
to be noted that the two poems which under their first titles,
'Excuse' and 'Indifference,' had in 1852 stood between two poems
which later became i and ii of 'Faded Leaves,' and which in 1855
had followed the 'Faded Leaves' group with only one intervening
poem ('Self-Deception'), are now, in 1869, completely separated from
their former associates and placed in a different volume; yet though
they follow immediately the 'Switzerland' group they precede 'Calais
Sands,' which is certified to Mrs. Arnold. In 1877 the *Poems,* a
"New and Complete Edition," were again issued in two volumes;
followed by a new edition of the same, in 1881, with one change
of interest here, the restoration of 'A Dream.'

    In the meantime Arnold had published his *Selected Poems,* 1878,
which was frequently reprinted. Here a section called Early Poems
was created, to which was relegated the former 'Switzerland i,' i.e.,

'To My Friends,' now renamed 'A Memory Picture.' The 'Switzerland' group now has taken its final form:

    i. Meeting ('The Lake,' 1852, 1853, 1854, 1857, 1869)
   ii. 'Parting' (1852, 1853, 1854, 1857, 1869)
  iii. 'A Farewell' (1852, 1854, 1857, 1869)
  iv. 'Isolation. To Marguerite' ["We were apart"] (1857, 1869)
   v. 'To Marguerite. Continued' ["Yes! in the Sea"] (1852, 1853,
      1854, 1857, 1869)
  vi. 'Absence' (1852, 1853, 1854, 1857, 1869)
 vii. 'The Terrace at Berne' (1867, 1869)

These poems were followed by 'The Strayed Reveller,' two excerpts
from 'Empedocles,' 'Urania,' 'Euphrosyne,' 'Calais Sands,' 'Dover
Beach,' etc. There were no 'Faded Leaves' poems in the *Selected
Poems*.

Finally, in 1885, appeared the Library Edition in three volumes
(followed in 1890 by the posthumous *Poetical Works* in one volume)
where for the first time since 1852, when the two groups were still
unnamed and unseparated, the 'Switzerland' and the 'Faded Leaves'
poems coexisted between the same covers. Volume I contains Early
Poems, Narrative Poems, and Sonnets—among them 'A Memory
Picture,' formally connected with the 'Switzerland' group by
Arnold's note to 'Meeting,' and followed by 'A Dream.' Volume II
contains the Lyric and Elegiac Poems, and begins with the seven
poems of the 'Switzerland' group, and after five intervening titles
come 'Urania,' 'Euphrosyne,' 'Calais Sands,' 'Faded Leaves' (which
had not been reprinted since 1869), 'Despondency,' 'Self-Deception,'
'Dover Beach,' etc.

Two generalizations may, within reason, be made. One is the
definite limitation of the Marguerite canon so far as Arnold wished
it to be recognized. Of the nine poems, all but two bear her name
either in the title or in the text; and of those two 'Absence' was with
the 'Switzerland' poems in their first untitled arrangement and thereafter always included in the group. The other, 'A Farewell,' was
distinctly separated from the group in 1852, was omitted in 1853,
and thereafter always included. One may infer therefore that
Arnold did not at first want it associated with Marguerite, but once
he decided there was no hesitation. (The possibility that it was

not written about her in the first instance, but added to her poems because of its similar content, need not be considered.) If any other poems were written for her or about her, Arnold has left no hint; and since he was so definite about the nine, criticism and speculation should be correspondingly cautious. Some have thought they saw her in 'The Voice'; for a long time she was supposed to be in 'Faded Leaves'; there is a Margaret in 'The Forsaken Merman'; there are blue eyes in 'Tristram and Iseult.' But all such attempted extensions of the canon are risky and gratuitous. I, for one, however, should like to include 'Destiny,' both because it was among the Marguerite poems in 1852 and if Arnold had chosen to reprint it it might well have remained among them, and also because its tone and meaning are consistent with them. For the rest, though the shifting positions are complicated in the explaining they show no sign of intentional concealment or (*pace* Professor Garrod) mystification. It has even been argued that "Arnold's frequent reconsideration of the content and order of the series suggests that references to Marguerite may be found elsewhere than in the 'Switzerland' group"; but reconsideration of the *order* of the series, which was frequent enough, need not be confused with reconsideration of the *content*. And such a remark as "I think I find her even in unlikely contexts" hardly commends itself to serious criticism. Arnold seems to have hesitated for a time about 'A Farewell' and he could not easily make up his mind about the position of 'A Memory Picture' and 'A Dream,' probably because of their lighter tone. But this is all.

The other conclusion is that Arnold clearly meant, after 1852, to keep the 'Switzerland' and 'Faded Leaves' poems apart. The former were always in his *First Series* and the latter in his *Second Series,* until the Collected Edition of 1869, and then they were in different volumes. He excluded 'Faded Leaves' from the *Selected Poems*. We know now that the 'Faded Leaves' poems were written to Miss Wightman and represent the early stages of his wooing of the *"unerreichbare schöne,"* and there is no point in canvassing the reasons, never plausible though characteristic of much Arnold criticism, why they ever were confused with the Marguerite poems. Within this group, however, is a point worth a moment's attention. In 1852 'Excuse' ('Urania') and 'Indifference' ('Euphrosyne') stood within the poems which in 1855 became 'Faded Leaves'; but in 1855 they followed 'Faded Leaves' with one intervening poem ('Self-Deception'). In 1869 they followed 'The Terrace at Berne' though they could not properly be read as related to it, and immediately preceded 'Calais Sands,' which was written for Miss Wightman, and 'Dover Beach,' which is usually associated with her. In 1878 (*Selected Poems*) there were three poems between them and 'The Terrace at Berne,' but they still immediately preceded 'Calais Sands' and 'Dover Beach'; and this volume did not contain 'Faded Leaves.' In 1885 there were five poems between them and 'The Terrace at Berne' and then the (final) order became: 'Urania,' 'Euphrosyne,' 'Calais Sands,' 'Faded Leaves,' 'Despondency,' 'Self-Deception,' 'Dover Beach.' The increasing separation between the last of the 'Switzerland' group and these two is probably not significant, but it does seem significant that when they were first printed they were surrounded by 'Faded Leaves' poems, next were separated only by 'Self-Deception,' and thereafter stood always just before 'Calais Sands.' Whatever else may be implied, I am inclined to believe that they were written about Miss Wightman.

Finally, it appears that these rearrangements afford no evidence for dating the composition of any of the poems beyond the obvious *terminus ad quem* of the date of publication.

6. 'Dover Beach'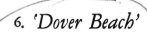

'DOVER BEACH,' one of Arnold's most admired poems, was probably composed in the summer of 1851 and subsequently revised for the volume of *New Poems* in 1867. The evidences for this date are tenuous, but taken together amount to reasonable probability. 'Dover Beach' has something in common with 'Philomela,' which was published in 1853: a pleasing melancholy (Arnold's phrase for 'The Scholar-Gipsy'), a similar structure (the setting, with moonlight, the story, the personal appeal to Eugenia), a contrast of the present and the Greek background, and somewhat of the same metrical form.[1] It has even more in common with 'Stanzas from the Grande Chartreuse,' which was begun in the autumn of 1851 and published in *Fraser's* for April 1855. The similarity here is the contrast between the Greek and a modern in their loss of faith. Either poem might have suggested the other in the comparable parts, but it is more likely that Arnold used the same idea in both at about the same time. (Bonnerot, pp. 369-71, has emphasized the parallels.)

[1] Eugenia appears first in 'Horatian Echo,' written in 1847, and again in 'Philomela,' which was written on the fly-leaf of a copy of Latham's *English Language,* London, 1848. Tinker and Lowry speak of her as "the poet's imaginary mistress" and as "probably a lay figure, like the lady addressed in the last paragraph of 'Dover Beach' " (*Commentary,* pp. 59, 164, 165, 59). In other words, nothing is known about her.

Nearly everyone assumes that 'Dover Beach' was written with Mrs. Arnold in mind; Tinker and Lowry are distinguished exceptions. In the 1867 volume it immediately followed 'Calais Sands' (though it was immediately followed by the Marguerite poem, 'The Terrace at Berne') and Sir E. K. Chambers says plainly *"Dover Beach* and *Calais Sands* are both related to *Faded Leaves."*[2] If one assumes further that the picture of Dover Beach in the moonlight—"Come to the window"— represents the stop of Arnold and his wife at Dover on their wedding journey in June 1851, there would be corroboration in the later lines

> *the world which seems*
> *To lie before us . . .*
> *So various, so beautiful, so new;*

and there would be additional poignancy in the appeal "let us be true To one another" in spite of all its hostile forces.

i

The poem consists of four sections or stanzas: the setting (1-14); Sophocles, or the Greek parallel (15-20); the sea at Dover and the Sea of Faith, or the parallel extended (21-28); and the personal appeal (29-37). The first two stanzas were

---

[2] E. K. Chambers, *Matthew Arnold, A Study.* Oxford, 1947, p. 59. There is a kind of factual corroboration in the meteorological data. Arnold was married on 10 June 1851. The moon was full about 7 P.M. on the thirteenth and rose at 6:49 P.M.; therefore on any evening of the week following his wedding he could have seen the moon lying "fair Upon the straits" at Dover. High water at London Bridge was at 0:35 A.M., 1:00 P.M.; at Dover it would be a little later. The *Gentleman's Magazine* for July 1851 reports the weather as "fair, rain" for 11-13 June and as "fine, do." for 14-17 June. To be sure, poets are not held accountable for meteorological exactitude; but the setting of 'Dover Beach' has a factual air, and if the poem was written in or of mid-June 1851 it seems clear that Arnold's details are correct.

written in pencil on the verso of a sheet of Arnold's notes for his 'Empedocles.' The third appears on the same sheet but at the side of the page: ". . . of the world. Ah love &c." This might suggest that the whole was put together out of three separate parts: the first twenty lines, the last nine lines, and the intervening eight lines added as a link. This would surprise no one in view of Arnold's early letter to his sister, "myself am fragments"; nor is it inconsistent with what one may suppose to be a common practice of poets. It suggested to Tinker and Lowry, however, that the concluding stanza was the first part written and the preceding twenty-eight lines added as a "prelude." In any case, there is an easy and natural movement from beginning to end of the finished poem, and with one reservation a sufficient consistency.

Nevertheless this movement is not altogether simple, as is evident from certain misunderstandings which readers and commentators have revealed.

The seascape—calm, high tide, the cliffs looking "vast" in the moonlight—gives the key. *But*[3] there is the beating of the surf, "the grating roar Of pebbles," the "tremulous cadence"[4] which adds "The eternal note of sadness" to the scene. As

[3] "Only" (line 7) must bear this meaning; it goes with the semi-colloquial tone of language and meter—up to the last stanza. The sea is calm, the night is still, except for . . . It results from Arnold's choice of his alternative epithets for "the night air." One of them, "hush'd," would have gone well with the first lines, but he chose the other, "sweet," probably as more appropriate with "Come to the window."

[4] *Tremulous*, for which the manuscript has *regular* with *mournful* as alternative, is an affective rather than a descriptive word. It occurs four times in Arnold's verse. It has descriptive value in 'The Strayed Reveller,' line 282:

> *Ah, the cool night-wind, tremulous stars!*
> *Ah, glimmering water,*
> *Fitful earth-murmur. . . .*

The echoes of this in 'Dover Beach' are interesting.

illustration that the note is eternal Arnold instances Sophocles, his favorite tragic poet. This same wash of the sea against the shore had made the same impression on Sophocles: it had reminded him, even as it reminds us in the north, of "the turbid ebb and flow Of human misery." Here one must be cautious. Arnold does not say that Sophocles compared the vicissitudes of life to the ebb and flow of the Aegean tides; nor has anyone ever found in the seven extant plays or in the numerous fragments any such comparison; nor was Sophocles likely to have made such a comparison, because there is little tide in the Aegean. The alleged parallels simply do not meet the case; they are irrelevant. In *Antigone* 583 ff. he compares the curse of heaven on a family to the Thracian sea-winds stirring up the sand and beating against the headlands. In *The Trachinian Maidens* 111 ff. he compares the changes in Heracles' life to the billow after billow of the storm winds. In *Oedipus at Colonus* he has the Chorus say that Oedipus is like a cape lashed by winds and waves. These and other passages may have been vaguely in Arnold's memory. They are, anyway, not strikingly original or recondite. Certainly they would not justify Arnold in saying what he has been supposed to say but did not say. For what Arnold says is that Sophocles, who knew the Aegean Sea, not the English Channel, hearing the surf beat on the shore felt the same sadness over the alternations of the human lot.[5] It is Arnold and not Sophocles who

[5] Since nothing has been adduced from Sophocles which at all resembles this "thought," viz., the alternations of joy and misery compared to the motion of waves on the shore, it is likely that Arnold chose the name—so much more definite than "a Greek" in the Grande Chartreuse poem—because Sophocles *was* his favorite tragic poet, "The mellow glory of the Attic stage." Any tragedy of course moves from prosperity to disaster, but not back and forth like the waves. Euripides might have been a better choice for accuracy, if a kind of melancholy pessimism is implied in the comparison, but not for sound or associative value.—A sort of parallel to Arnold's use of Sophocles has been suggested

uses the metaphor of the tides, a metaphor suggested by the view and sound from his window at Dover.

Perhaps "metaphor of the tides" is itself a misleading phrase, for there is only one tide in the text of the poem, the full or high tide. But most readers (like Tinker and Lowry: "the ebb and flow of the sea at Dover") have been led astray by "ebb and flow Of human misery." Perhaps Arnold is partly responsible for the confusion, and one or two words require special attention. There is no difficulty with "it":

> Sophocles long ago
> Heard it on the Ægæan—

heard the "tremulous cadence slow," the rhythm of the waves breaking and drawing back. This ordinarily we see rather than hear, but the time is night and on a pebbly beach there is a "grating roar" or at least a distinct noise as the waves withdraw; and this Arnold likens to the larger movement of the ebb and flow of tides. In line 8 the manuscript had

> *Where the sea meets the moon-blanched sand.*

The last word was changed in 1880 to "land," obviously to avoid the inconsistency of sand and pebbles ("shingles," line 28). But for "sea" the first printing, 1867, had "ebb," which remained through three editions and was not changed to "sea" until 1880. This is of course an improvement, for at Dover, *in the poem,* the sea is always at high tide. But the idea was present in Arnold's mind and appears nine lines below in "ebb and flow Of human misery," which is still not tides but the forward and retreating movement of waves on the beach.

The sound of this movement produces in "us" at Dover

---

to me in Keats' use of Ruth in 'Ode to a Nightingale.' Both Sophocles and Ruth carry the reader back in time, and as there is nothing in the Greek texts about "the ebb and flow Of human misery," so there is no nightingale in the *Book of Ruth.*

"a thought"—presumably that of the next stanza, namely, that Faith, which was once like a full tide, has now ebbed. So that now, in imagination

> *I only hear*
> *Its melancholy, long, withdrawing roar,*
> *Retreating.*

The two images, the ebb and flow of waves and the ebb and flow of tides are blended, or rather, the one is imaginatively extended to become the other; and

> *the grating roar*
> *Of pebbles which the waves draw back*

is transformed to the retreating movement of the tide, as the Sea of Faith recedes. Arnold does not see and hear this literally; he expands the metaphor, just as he enlarges the surf at Dover to include

> *the vast edges drear*
> *And naked shingles of the* [whole] *world.*

There is another small difficulty:

> *The Sea of Faith*
> *Was once, too, at the full;*

that is, *as* the actual tide at Dover is now high, *so* the Sea of Faith was at one time in the past at high tide; but not now. This does not mean, as it might mean, that in the time of Sophocles the Sea of Faith was at high tide. The word "too" does not refer to the fifth century B.C., but to the Dover tide in, say, 1851. Perhaps it is not supersubtle to see in "too" also an anticipation of the concluding stanza: we, Arnold and his bride, were full of faith when we married, and may we remain so in spite of the "confused alarms" which we shall presently face. "Let us be true To one another!" through the darkness and joylessness of the world before us. The sequence of images,

feelings, and ideas is thus simple and natural and with reasonable care not difficult to follow.

But Arnold was not content with this; his weakness for
ending on a high note was too strong for him.[6]   In the last
three lines he brought in a new image, apparently to intensify
the dark picture of human misery but confusing and inappropriate because, as everyone feels, it shifts our interest and
attention from the sea imagery, which has been dominant
hitherto, to one of "a darkling plain, Where ignorant armies
clash by night."   This is the one structural blemish of the poem.

The critics have also darkened counsel by their search for
sources.   For the sea of faith we are referred to a passage in
Sainte-Beuve; and this is interesting at least because it was noted
by three different readers independently.[7]   Sainte-Beuve, who
was of course one of Arnold's favorite authors, set down, near
Aigues-Mortes, on the Gulf of Lyons, in 1839 this *pensée:*

Mon âme est pareille à ces plages où l'on dit que saint Louis s'est
embarqué: la mer et la foi se sont depuis longtemps, helas! retirées,
et c'est tout si parfois, à travers les sables, sous l'aride chaleur ou le
froid mistral, je trouve un instant à m'asseoir à l'ombre d'un rare
tamarin.[8]

This may safely be regarded as a parallel 'thought'—the sea
and faith have, alas, long since withdrawn—rather than one
which gave Arnold the necessary hint for his poem or even two
lines of it.

[6] This would be true, in a slightly different sense, if the last stanza
was written before the rest; for in putting the parts together Arnold
allowed the disturbing metaphor to stand.

[7] Clarence C. Clark, "A Possible Source of Matthew Arnold's *Dover
Beach,*" *MLN,* xvii (1902), 484-85; Arnold Whitridge, "Matthew
Arnold and Sainte-Beuve," *PMLA,* liii (1935), 303-13; 307-308, with
no reference to Clark; I. E. Sells, *Matthew Arnold and France. The
Poet,* Cambridge, 1935, who got it from Babbitt, *Masters of Modern
French Criticism,* New York, 1912, p. 104.

[8] *Portraits littéraires,* new ed., Paris 1864, iii, 540.

A fragment of Empedocles is of interest only because the last stanza of 'Dover Beach' is found among Arnold's notes for his 'Empedocles on Etna.' It will hardly be taken as a source or even as a suggestion for the battle imagery of the stanza. The most that could be urged is that it might have reminded him of the passage in Thucydides. It has been translated as follows: "The joyless land where are Murder and Wrath and the tribes of other Dooms, and Wasting Diseases and Corruptions and the Works of Dissolution wander over the Meadow of Disaster in the darkness."[9]

In 413 B.C. the Athenians and their Greek allies brought a fleet to Sicily and in the attack on Syracuse engaged the enemy on the hill of Epipolae. "Now it seemed impossible," Thucydides narrates;

Now it seemed impossible to approach the heights in the daytime . . . and after the first watch, . . . they got by the Syracusan guards without being observed, . . . and killed some of the guards; most of these, however, fled at once to the camps, of which there were three upon Epipolae . . . and brought word of the attack, informing also the six hundred Syracusans who were posted as an advanced guard. . . . These hastened at once to the rescue, but Demosthenes and the Athenians met them and put them to rout despite their vigorous resistance. This body of Athenians then straightway pressed forward . . . ; while another party at the very first proceeded to seize the cross-wall of the Syracusans, ... But the Syracusans and their allies . . . came up from the outworks; yet, since this daring attempt had been made upon them unexpectedly at night, they were still dazed as they attacked the Athenians and were at first forced back by them. But while the Athenians were by now going forward, in some disorder, considering themselves victorious and wishing as quickly as possible to push their way through all the enemy's forces that had not yet been engaged, . . . it was the Boeotians who first made a stand against them, and by making a charge routed and put them to flight.

[9] Kathleen Freeman, *Ancilla to The Pre-Socratic Philosophers,* Oxford, 1946; Empedocles, Fragment 121.

XLIV. By this time the Athenians were getting into a state of so great confusion and perplexity that it has not been easy to learn from either side just how the several events occurred . . . . in a battle by night—the only one that took place in this war between large armies—how could anyone know anything clearly? For though there was a bright moon, they could only see one another, as it is natural to do in moonlight—seeing before them the vision of a person but mistrusting their recognition of their own friends. There were, besides, large numbers of hoplites belonging to both sides moving about in a narrow space. And on the Athenian side, some were already defeated, while others, still in their first onset, were advancing unchecked; but of the rest of the army a large portion had only just finished the ascent and others were still coming up, so that they did not know which body to join. For the front lines were already all in confusion in consequence of the rout that had taken place, and the two sides were difficult to distinguish by reason of the outcries. The Syracusans and their allies, as they were winning, were cheering one another and indulging in no little shouting—it being impossible in the night to communicate in any other way—while at the same time they held their ground against their assailants; the Athenians were trying to find their own comrades, and regarded as hostile what came from the opposite direction, even though it might be a party of friends belonging to the troops already in flight, and as they were constantly calling out the demand for the watchword, the only means they had of distinguishing friend from foe, they not only caused much confusion in their own ranks, everybody making the demand at the same time, but also made their watchword known to the enemy. . . . [etc., etc.] . . . And so finally, when once they had been thrown into confusion, coming into collision with their own comrades in many different parts of the army, friends with friends and citizens with fellow-citizens, they not only became panicstricken but came to blows with one another and were with difficulty separated. And as they were being pursued by the enemy many hurled themselves down from the bluffs and perished. . . .[10]

There is every reason to suppose, though no positive evi-

[10] Thucydides, VII, xliii-xliv. Trans. Charles F. Smith, Loeb ed., London 1923, iv, 83-91.

dence, that Arnold had read Thucydides at Rugby. (His father
had edited the *History*, 1830-35.) And this passage is the most
likely source, if a source must be found, for the closing image
of 'Dover Beach.' He need not have returned to the text; a
general recollection of the story would have been enough.
Clough used a similar reference in 'The Bothie,' but Arnold,
unlike Clough, did not include the "watchword," and he substituted "darkling plain" (as though to suit with the setting at
Dover) for the hill of Epipolae; but the rest, the tone and the
confusion of armies, is all there in Thucydides.[11]

ii

The meter of 'Dover Beach,' for all its apparent simplicity
and ease, is more subtle than one might think. The four
stanzas differ in length, but the second and third together
(which form a unit of meaning, a contrast to the first stanza),
are of the same length as the first. Line 9 of the first stanza has
to wait till the third stanza for its answering rime (*roar : shore
: roar*). The fourth stanza repeats the rime word *light* (lines 3,
33) and so the *a*-rimes of the first stanza. In this way the first
two and the last stanzas are interlinked by rime. There is some
parallelism in the arrangement of rimes. The opening pattern
aba recurs as *dbd* and *gfg* in the first stanza, and carries over
to the second stanza: *aba cbc*. The third stanza differs from
all the others. The fourth is the most regular and goes something like the octave of a sonnet: *abba cddc,* plus the last rime,

[11] It has been supposed that Arnold took the incident from Clough
rather than direct from the Greek. See Paul Turner, *"Dover Beach
and the Bothie of Tober-na-Vuolich," English Studies,* XXVIII (1947),
173-78. The idea is that Arnold disagreed with the wishful thinking
of the *'Bothie'* and composed a fragment of nine lines to express his
disagreement; but withheld the (finished) poem till 1867 lest Clough
(d. 1861) should be offended. See also Buckner B. Trawick, "The Sea
of Faith and the Battle by Night in *Dover Beach." PMLA,* LXV (1950),
1282-83.

c, repeated with a kind of coda effect. It need not be supposed that these are all carefully contrived devices, but they contribute to, as they offset, the seemingly natural flow of the whole poem. The variations in length of line are similarly subtle. Measured by stresses, the first runs 345 555 444 5454 4; the second 355 345; the third 255 353 54; the fourth consists of seven 5-stress lines introduced by a 3-stress and concluded by a 4-stress line. All four stanzas begin with a short line: 3, 3, 2, 3. Three of the four stanzas end with a 4-stress line. The 555 444 54 54 grouping of the first stanza is echoed by the 54 endings of the third and fourth stanzas. Moreover, twenty of the thirty-seven lines as printed are 5-stress lines; but besides these there are several examples of concealed blank verse:

> *The sea is calm to-night. The tide is full*
> *on the French coast the light Gleams and is gone*
> *the cliffs of England stand, Glimmering and vast*
> *and fling, At their return, up the high strand*
> *and bring The eternal note of sadness in.*
> *The Sea of Faith Was once, too, at the full*
> *Retreating to the breath Of the night-wind*
> *Ah, love, let us be true To one another!*

Others might pass as blank verse:

> *Listen! you hear the grating roar Of pebbles*
> *the turbid ebb and flow Of human misery.*

Or this last could be read as an alexandrine, and so also

> *With tremulous cadence slow and bring The eternal note*
> *Sophocles long ago Heard it on the Ægean*
> *which seems To lie before us like a land of dreams.*

These combinations or variations confirm the smoothness of the rhythm alongside the apparent irregularity of the line-length;[12] and at the same time the interweaving of shorter and

[12] The meter of 'Philomela' is less varied. Of its thirty-two lines,

longer lines produces something of the effect of waves breaking
and retreating, of "ebb and flow."

---

five are 2-stress, eleven are 3-stress, and eleven are 5-stress.   Lines 1-2
and 14-15 together make blank verse and there are two concealed in

> *And can this fragrant lawn With its cool trees*
> *and feel come over thee, Poor fugitive.*

The poem is ostensibly unrimed, but two lines (4 and 8) end with *pain*
and two (7 and 14) with *brain;* and lines 23, 26 have a conventional
rime (*thee* : *agony*).

7. 'The Buried Life'

INTRINSICALLY, as a poem, 'The Buried Life' does not deserve much attention. But its faults are interesting and its subjects are Arnoldian favorites.

The 98 lines of the poem are divided in the printing into eight or nine unequal paragraphs (the editions vary and in some there are additional indentions), but it falls into three main parts: 1-29, 30-76, 77-98. The first eleven lines are addressed to a beloved; then for twelve lines the poet addresses himself; then in a couplet he turns to her again, and the last four lines of this section form a kind of conclusion which may also be regarded as a kind of transition to the next.

Let us be serious and silent awhile, he says to her, so that I can understand your inmost soul.—But alas, even love will not make the heart speak clearly. I knew that men were reluctant to reveal their thoughts, although

> *The same heart beats in every human breast!*

Is it so with us too?—It is well for us (we are lucky) if we can even for a moment speak freely; for what seals our lips has been "deep-ordain'd."

The tone—"mocking words" and her "light words" and "gay smiles"—suggests Marguerite; the repetitions "Yes, yes," "We know, we know" betray Arnold's earlier manner; and so one may agree with Tinker and Lowry (p. 195) that there is "an obvious relation, in its opening motive, to the Marguerite series," namely, the motive of isolation. Isolation, however, has two senses. The isolation he felt with Marguerite was that of complete severance: even "their longing's fire" cannot bring the lovers together. Here he is troubled by the feeling that love cannot break down the barriers of communication. M. Bonnerot (p. 77) is confident that he sees Marguerite here. He quotes two irrelevant lines from 'A Farewell,' a Marguerite poem which immediately followed 'The Buried Life' in 1852; and also (but inaccurately) two lines from 'Parting,' another Marguerite poem, which offer a real parallel:

> *And what heart knows another?*
> *Ah! who knows his own?*[1]

Tinker and Lowry find also an "obvious relation . . . in the

[1] Not much can be gathered from Arnold's shifting positions of these poems. 'The Buried Life' appeared first in *Empedocles on Etna and Other Poems*, 1852, preceded by 'A Summer Night' and followed by 'A Farewell' and the first Obermann 'Stanzas.' It was not in the New Edition of 1853, reprinted in 1854 and 1857. It was reprinted however in *Poems. Second Series*, 1855, preceded by the Obermann 'Stanzas' and followed by 'The Youth of Nature,' 'The Youth of Man,' and 'A Summer Night.' (This volume contained no Marguerite poems.) It did not appear, naturally, in the *New Poems* of 1867, 1868. But in the two-volume *Poems* of 1869 it reappeared (in vol. II) preceded by 'Switzerland,' 'Urania,' 'Euphrosyne,' 'Calais Sands,' 'Dover Beach,' and followed by the group of 'Sonnets.' In vol. II of the three-volume Library Edition it found its final position, towards the end of the Lyric Poems section, well separated from both 'Switzerland' and 'Faded Leaves,' but now preceded by 'A Summer Night' (as originally in 1852), and followed by the Kensington Gardens 'Lines.' It was not reprinted in the *Selections*, 1878. Its first and final positions were next to 'A Summer Night,' one of the many *unrest* poems, with the confessional

> *Never by passion quite possess'd*
> *And never quite benumb'd by the world's sway*

(put as a rhetorical question). It was sometimes in a Marguerite context, and once stood beside two poems associated with Mrs. Arnold.

second half, to 'Dover Beach,'" which preceded it in 1869. This is more difficult to accept. But, while one admits that it is unnecessary and probably uncritical to attach 'The Buried Life' to any particular lady, one might, if so inclined, assume a biographical place for it, as a composite piece, with the remembered unsatisfactory Marguerite situation at the beginning and the happier situation with Mrs. Arnold at the close. The main section on the frustration theme would represent Arnold's indecisions in the late 1840's, and "the interminable hours" might possibly reflect his impatience with school inspecting later. The admission, "but this is rare" (77), is perhaps less than complimentary, but we know that his decision in 1851 left him more resigned than reconciled. And if there is something of 'Dover Beach' in 'The Buried Life,' the link might be Mrs. Arnold.

The poem continues: its next fifteen lines (30-44), a single sentence, introduce a new subject. Fate, foreseeing that we might dissipate our true being too readily, ordained that there should be within us, like a river flowing beneath the surface of our life, a restraining force to keep us true to ourselves.—But the figure (like the pronouns: "man . . . his . . . him . . . our") is very confused. This river, which is not presented in a simile but in a direct statement, is not only "buried," it is "indiscernible" and "unregarded" and unseen; therefore it is difficult to understand how it could prevent us from straying, losing our identity, giving way to caprice, while we "seem to be Eddying at large"—the first reading was "Eddying about." The metaphor remains fluid, but puzzling. For we now seem to be moving on the surface of a river which runs "through the deep recesses of our breast."

The next paragraph (45-76) continues: But often, though that river is unseen and unregarded, we desire "knowledge of our buried life." *Buried* implies something finished and put away or something deliberately and carefully hidden. The river, however, was buried in a quite different sense; it was something which Fate had placed underground, out of sight, though (seemingly) to act as a restraining influence on our natural capriciousness—a little like the tutelary spirit, say, in 'The Scholar-Gipsy.' But often, Arnold goes on, not only do we desire knowledge of our buried life, we also feel "A thirst to spend our fire" (a mixed metaphor) in discovering our true nature, in expressing the mystery of our hearts, the source of our "thoughts" (altered in 1881 to "lives"). We delve and mine into our breast, as though to find that subterranean river.—The attentive and sympathetic reader now begins to glimpse a faint clue to the hidden relationship of ideas. We have erred, we have strayed from our true selves, we have been unable to express ourselves; we have tried "to act Our hidden self," but in vain.

This takes us through line 66. To recapitulate. Love is, or at least sometimes is, incapable of breaking through the barrier of communication; even between lovers there is an element of reserve. Yet there is an undercurrent of instinctive power which should guide us, help us to know ourselves, to be ourselves, to express ourselves. It cannot be claimed that Arnold has done much to help the reader in pursuing these involutions. It might be said that he has symbolically illustrated the difficulties of self-expression. Not the lover, not even the Muse, can achieve clarity and coherence in language. Life is difficult and obscure; therefore the criticism of life which is poetry shall be difficult and obscure.

"And then," he continues, omitting the logical connective but meaning to say: then, if we do succeed in speaking and acting our hidden self—

> *And then we will be no more rack'd*
> *With inward striving, and demand*

Of all the thousand nothings of the hour
Their stupefying power;
Ah yes, and they benumb us at our call!

—then we are determined to be ("will" in the volitional sense)
racked no longer by those inward strivings, and we take refuge
in momentary distractions which, when we call upon them,
stupefy and benumb our better selves.

Yet still, from time to time . . .

He was saving *yet* for this last turn of the screw. We try to
be ourselves, we almost succeed, though not quite, and yet
sometimes we hear echoes from that land far beneath us
through which runs our subterranean river, and those echoes
leave us melancholy because they certify our failures. (Again
Arnold might almost be describing his poem.)

Only—but this is rare—

he continues, in the third and final section (77-98)—and "Only"
means both *however,* the strong prepositive adversative, and
also *solely, exclusively.* Only when jaded by those distractions,
do we experience the miracle of love, only on such rare oc-
casions does love renew us and reveal us to ourselves and
make us articulate; in a word, bring us into relation with that
mysterious river, no longer subterranean, but winding mur-
murously through open meadows, in open sunlight. *Then—*
but his word is "And"—we are calmed and comforted, and
think we understand the meaning of our life. "Think" is a
melancholy concession to overconfidence. Thus the fundamental image, which at first lurked in "the deep recesses of
our breast," has come finally, and with the reader's explicatory
aid, to the surface. The Hidden River (which is the only
proper title for the poem) has, in spite of its "winding
murmur," come clear.

After the river image, the next ranking figure is *breast*. This word occurs in rime six times—three times with *rest* (6, 7; 23, 21; 95, 93), once with *possess'd* (38, 32), once with *unexpress'd* (62, 63), and once with *caress'd* (84, 83). Within the line it occurs once. The variety of adjunct images, moreover, is considerable. There are the chains which seal our lips (28-29), the *lines* (57-60) which are our right track to follow (and which may perhaps be associated with the new railways), the feelings which course through our breast (62-63), the strivings which rack us and the distractions which benumb us (67-71), our eyes which see clearly when our ears hear a loved voice (81-83), the bolt shot back in our [overworked] breast (84), the hot race with its lull (91), the flying shadow of rest (93). All these and some lesser ones, with their rapid accumulation in the latter half of the poem, are superimposed upon—they cannot be said to be amalgamated with—the dominant image of a river. They afford an embarrassment of wealth, all kinds of ore in every rift.

To a poet familiar with the Thames at Richmond, the Isis at Oxford, the river image, though banal enough, was also natural enough. It appeared first in Arnold's poetry in his Oxford prize poem 'Cromwell':

> *Till life, unstirr'd by action, life became ...*
> *Like a swift river thro' a silent plain.*
>
> . . . .
>
> *Then—like a kindly river—swift and strong*
> *The future roll'd its gathering tides along!*

In the early Marguerite poem, 'A Dream,' the "green Alpine stream" was transformed into

> *The darting river of Life*
> *(Such now, methought, it was), the river of Life,*
> *Loud thundering.*

In 'To a Gipsy Child by the Sea-Shore' (a blend of Gray and Wordsworth) the child ends on her "storm-vext stream of life." In 'Progress,' the penultimate poem of the 'Empedocles' volume, 1852, there is a rolling "stream of life," and 'The Future,' which immediately followed, closing the volume, has "the river of Time" for its leitmotif. In the later poem, 'Epilogue to Lessing's Laocoön,' there are the souls on whom

> *The stream of life's majestic whole*

had never been mirrored. There are of course other rivers, the Nile in 'Mycerinus,' the Rhine in 'Faded Leaves,' and the majestic Oxus in 'Sohrab.' The stream, says Empedocles in his long craggy ode,

> *The stream, like us, desires*
> *An unimpeded way.*

But the poem in which Arnold most successfully employs the river image is the early 'In Utrumque Paratus,' a poem whose studied concinnity stands in strong contrast to the diffuseness of 'The Buried Life.'

> *O waking on a world which thus-wise springs!*
> *Whether it needs thee count*
> *Betwixt thy waking and the birth of things*
> *Ages or hours—O waking on life's stream!*
> *By lonely pureness to the all-pure fount*
> *(Only by this thou canst) the colour'd dream*
> *Of life remount!*

This poem is *wrought*. Arnold took pains with it. It has its blemishes, it is not altogether lucid, but it shows throughout that he tried; and that is more than can be said for 'The Buried Life.'

For with more applied effort than Arnold chose to lay out, 'The Buried Life' might have been one of his better poems. It appears to contain a good idea, the hidden river which is the guide of our true life if we only would recognize it; and to this is added a love motif, that true love will help us to find it and follow its course. But he has overloaded this dual theme with extraneous momenta and obscured it with too many strained and unassimilable metaphors. By an act of supererogation, the explicator may reduce the chaos somewhat, but the poem itself, as Arnold printed and reprinted it, is less a tribute to the Muses than a monument of his "still vex'd" spirit in 1850, or a little later, when he was wrestling with the world, the flesh, and the devil and could not come to terms with himself. It is a kind of portent, a sign that he was yielding to the lower Trinity and unequal to the demands of the dedicated life of a poet. And what strikes one most unhappily after the complexities of the text have been mastered, is that the love motif which serves as a framework and seems from its introductory and concluding position to be significant is entirely secondary. At first love is inadequate to what he asks; at the end it is a qualified success; and what the lady may have thought or felt does not interest him.

It is well understood that Arnold was deficient in self-criticism. As Dr. Lowry has observed, he could give us the felicities of 'Dover Beach' and the atrocities of some of the 1867 sonnets. He knew enough to be dissatisfied with Part II of 'Tristram and Iseult'; he seems not to have understood what he achieved and what he missed in 'Empedocles.' He was notoriously impercipient about *Merope;* and even in prose he could go strangely wrong with overconfidence as well as be wisely right. His sensitiveness to the touchstones in others' poetry forsook him when he regarded his own. He could master at times the succinct 'press' style; he could also be flat, prosaic, and banal, sometimes in the same poem. Many of the Obermann stanzas are doggerel; there are parts of 'Empedocles' which are wonderfully subtle in both phrasing and meter.

Considering his earnestness, one can hardly say that he did not care enough. Remembering his insistence on architectonics, one finds it difficult to overlook the lack of "fundamental brainwork" in many of his otherwise rewarding poems. His good is as unpredictable as his bad.

And here, no doubt, is the primary fault in the working out of 'The Buried Life.' The five lines which he first printed in "St. Paul and Protestantism" in the *Cornhill* for November 1869, may well have been the germ of this poem.[2]

> *Below the surface stream, shallow and light,*
> *Of what we say we feel—below the stream,*
> *As light, of what we think we feel—there flows*
> *With noiseless current strong, obscure and deep,*
> *The central stream of what we feel indeed.*

This is like a prose note cast into the semblance of blank verse, without felicity of expression; but it contains the apparently chief ingredient of 'The Buried Life,' with more probability of imagery. For here the stream, which reflects our surface feeling and speaking, has an undercurrent which represents our real feeling.

If these lines are the starting point of 'The Buried Life,' they reveal what is evident on a close view of the poem: that its theme is the contrast between our superficial life, which is "alien" to ourselves, and the "hidden self" which we disguise for fear of the indifference or reproof of others. To this was added what was most important to Arnold in c. 1850, the difficulty of knowing just what that hidden self is. One has melancholy inklings of it, but no certainty. This difficulty he

---

[2] The lines are introduced, with no indication of their origin, apropos (or inapropos) of Paul's doctrine of the resurrection. "Very likely it would have been impossible to him to imagine his theology without it. But:—[the five lines] and by this alone are we truly characterized." The implication would seem to be that Paul did not really believe his doctrine.

expands in the longest and most personal paragraph of the poem (45-76). To these two motifs are further added the potential of love—his love for Marguerite in 1849 and his love for Frances Lucy in 1851—to release the doubts and relieve the difficulties, *both* of communion of souls *and* of self-knowledge. The potential is realized, yes, but rarely, and then only partially: "then he thinks he knows" (96). It was a desperate hopefulness. The revelation was less than perfect: Arnold was at the crossroads, and either turning led to doubt for his tormented breast.

Such is the complex theme, into which is intertwined, from line 38 onwards, the hidden river with its "noiseless current strong" and with all its accompanying imagery "obscure and deep" and the other complicating imagery, as the "buried stream" rises, or seems to rise, out of the darkness to the sunlit meadows. Is it any wonder the result is obscure? The wonder is that Arnold did so well as he did, leaving the poor explicator to disentangle the threads. A general clarity was out of the question; for the confusion in the poem is the confusion in Arnold's mind.

8. *The Two Laments*

T̵ʜᴀᴛ 'The Scholar-Gipsy' and 'Thyrsis' are meant to be recognized as companion pieces and that Arnold hoped in 'Thyrsis' to repeat the success of 'The Scholar-Gipsy' are obvious enough; but there are a few similarities between them which are not altogether obvious.

i

The stanza seems to have been original with Arnold. It has some likeness with that of Keats' 'To a Nightingale,' which goes *ababcde⁵c³de⁵*, and is a kind of truncated sonnet with the eighth line shortened. Arnold's form is more subtle, for it has two different quatrains (*bcbc and deed*) and the shortened line is nearer the middle to give a neater balance. Further, the sixth or shortened line riming with the first (*abcbc⁵a³*) seems to make the first six lines a finished unit and to divide the stanza into two separate parts, yet does not, and thus the ear is pleasingly deceived. For only in three stanzas of the twenty-five of 'The Scholar-Gipsy' and in five of the twenty-four of 'Thyrsis' is there a full stop at the end of the sixth line, and in only seven more in the former poem and four more in the latter is there a strong pause there.

A very special device of Arnold's is the break at the end

of the first line of the stanzas. In 'The Scholar-Gipsy' there is a strong pause at the end of the first line in six stanzas and a full stop in eight others. In 'Thyrsis' there is a strong pause in one stanza and a full stop in ten others.

A stylistic peculiarity of both poems (though Arnold is fond of it elsewhere) is the number of lines beginning with "And." 'The Scholar-Gipsy' has 54 such lines of the total 250. There are only two stanzas without them; three stanzas have five of them. The proportion is less in 'Thyrsis'; it has only 35 such lines out of the total 240 lines. So also for lines beginning with "But"; 9 in the one and 7 in the other. (This is probably a quasi-Homeric trick, strongly favored in 'Sohrab,' with an increased frequency of "But" in 'Balder Dead.') 'Thyrsis,' however, compensates by the number of exclamation points. There are only four of its twenty-four stanzas without one (in the final printing) and one stanza (16) has seven of them! But in 'Thyrsis' Arnold was deliberately forcing the note.

There are no standards for the frequency of repeated rimes or rime-pairs in English poetry and no statistics on which a statement of custom might be based. Pope made easy fun of the easy rime *breeze : trees* (it actually occurs in 'Thyrsis'); Swinburne is noted for his very numerous repetitions, which are often defensible for their tonal effect. In the rimes of 'The Scholar-Gipsy' there is little remarkable. *Away* occurs four times in rime (three times with [*to-*]*day*) and *stray* three times; altogether there are eight pairs on this sound, besides *delays : days*. In 'Thyrsis' there are five pairs, besides *days : ways* and *strays : days*. Many of the same words but not the same pairs recur in the two poems. In 'The Scholar-Gipsy' the *be, he,* etc., rimes occur in seven pairs, three times relying on the suffix *-ly*. These occur only five times in 'Thyrsis' (*thee : see* twice). In 'The Scholar-Gipsy' *powers : ours* occurs twice, along with *hours* : *powers, showers* : *towers,* and *flowers* : *bowers;* whereas in 'Thyrsis' we have *power* : *hour,* three times. In 'The Scholar-Gipsy' *laid* : *shade* occurs twice, along with *shade* : *glade* and *made* : *fade;* but in 'Thyrsis' only *shade* : *invade* and *made* : *assay'd.*

In both poems there are the usual approximate or conventional rimes, but more in the former. In 'The Scholar-Gipsy' there are *borne* : *corn, o'ergrown* : *gone, flown* : *gone, foam* : *come, one* : *throne, knew* : *too, wood* : *solitude;* and in both poems *come* : *home.* In both poems *again* has both pronunciations (: *brain,* : *men,* : *train*). The irregular rimes in 'Thyrsis' are *farm* : *warm, on* : *snapdragon, throng* : *among, trees* : *orchises, trees* : *lattices.* The rime of *Thames* with *aims* has poetical precedent; *fritillaries* : *tributaries* calls for the older accentuation *fritíllaries.* The repeated pairs in 'Thyrsis' are *yields* : *fields* four times (once in consecutive stanzas), *to-night* : *bright, time* : *prime,* besides *power* : *hour* three times and *home* : *come* already mentioned.

Particularly interesting are the repetitions of rimes from one poem to the other. The first rime word in 'The Scholar-Gipsy' *hill* (: *still*) is echoed by the first rimes in 'Thyrsis' *fills* : *hills;* and *hill* : *still* are also the *e*-rimes of the last stanza of 'Thyrsis.' Many single rime words are repeated from poem to poem, but there are twelve pairs which occur in both: *fills* : *hills, strays* : *days, flames* : *Thames, power(s)* : *hour(s), rest* : *unblest, quest* : *rest, yields* : *fields, day* : *May, day* : *grey, days* : *ways, home* : *come, still* : *hill.*

Twice in 'The Scholar-Gipsy' Arnold repeats his rimes within the stanza; only once in 'Thyrsis.' In the former, stanza 4, the eye-rimes *poor* : *door* are repeated in *-lore* : *more;* and in stanza 12 the *b*-rimes *way* : *grey* are repeated as *e*-rimes *stray* : *spray.* Moreover, the *a*-rimes *delays* : *days* of stanza 19 echo the *e*-rimes *away* : *to-day* of the preceding stanza. In stanza 17 of

'Thyrsis' the *a*-rimes *veil* : *hail* are repeated as the *d*-rimes *vale* : *pale* with the enhancement of echo rime in *veil* : *vale*. Also, in stanza 20 there is particularly close assonance between the *a*-rimes *here* : *clear* and the *b*-rimes *despair* : *air*.

In brief: Arnold plays a few favorites in his choice of rimes for both poems, notably the rimes to *day,* etc., in both. Some of the repetitions from one poem to the other must be deliberate, some of them due to chance, and some due to the similarity of subject or setting.

There is one parallel of larger structure which the two poems have in common. Between the thirteenth and fourteenth stanzas of 'The Scholar-Gipsy,' or just past midway, there is a change or 'turn'—

> *But what—I dream! Two hundred years are flown. . . .*

In 'Thyrsis' this 'turn' comes also between the thirteenth and fourteenth stanzas, just past midway—

> *Yes, thou art gone! and round me too the night. . . .*

This is certainly not chance.

ii

The differences between the two poems are no less interesting. Some readers hold a preference for one, some for the other. There can be no question that in composing 'Thyrsis' Arnold labored under several handicaps. 'The Scholar-Gipsy' is so to say an original poem; he started fresh with it. 'Thyrsis' has the disadvantage of being a sequel.

When Clough died in November 1861 Arnold refused to write a formal obituary. He probably began his poem in the following year, but progress was slow and apparently he had not finished it till just before its publication in *Macmillan's Magazine* for April 1866. He produced, as he said, the only

tribute he was able to make. Meanwhile he had spoken of
Clough at the end of the lectures *On Translating Homer,*
November 1861.[1] Along with this sense of obligation to celebrate the death of his old friend there was also "my desire to
deal again with the Cumner country" or to write "a new poem
about the Cumner hillside, and Clough in connection with it."
The return to the Oxford landscape brought with it a repetition of certain ideas and phrases from 'The Scholar-Gipsy,'—
"the stripling Thames," which becomes "the youthful
Thames"; "the Fyfield elm," which haunts the later poem;
and the dual quest, the imaginary quest for the lost Scholar
and Arnold's own quest for his lost youth. The traditional

---

[1] The public mention of Clough was perhaps enough; to praise "the
Homeric simplicity of his literary life" does by itself sound faint and,
perhaps as the *Commentary* has it: "Just what Arnold meant to imply
by these words is not altogether easy to say" (p. 214). But simplicity
was in Arnold's view one of Homer's greatest qualities and the phrase
is at least complimentary. There is also a little more. In the third
lecture *On Translating Homer* he had praised the *'Bothie'* for "the
rapidity of its movement, and the plainness and directness of its style."
Then at the very end of the *Last Words* he turns from the successful
translation of Homer to the ideal study of Homer.

"And how, then, can I help being reminded what a student of
this sort we have just lost in Mr. Clough. . . . He, too, was busy
with Homer; but it is not on that account that I now speak of him.
Nor do I speak of him in order to call attention to his qualities and
powers in general, admirable as these were. I mention him because,
in so eminent a degree, he possessed these two invaluable literary
qualities,—a true sense for his object of study, and a single-hearted
care for it. He had both. . . . His interest was in literature itself;
and it was this which gave so rare a stamp to his character, which
kept him from all taint of littleness. . . . He had not yet traduced
his friends, nor flattered his enemies, nor disparaged what he admired, nor praised what he despised. . . . His poem, of which I
have spoken, has some admirable Homeric qualities. . . . But that
in him of which I think oftenest is the Homeric simplicity of his
literary life."

In context, therefore, Arnold's tribute is to an eminent degree clear
and proper.

elements of Greek pastoral elegy were of course more fitting than in 'The Scholar-Gipsy,' but on the other hand the relations between Clough and Arnold in their Oxford days had changed in the intervening fifteen years or so and the change had rendered the subject difficult and, one cannot help feeling, in many ways uncongenial. Certainly it is to Arnold's credit that he recognized this limitation of imperfect sympathy and refused to force his tribute beyond what he conscientiously felt. The charge was made—and accepted by Arnold—that the poem contained too little Clough. The corollary is also true: too much Arnold.

iii

Commentators, learned and amateur, have worried over the *tree* of both poems, and some have even doubted whether Arnold knew an elm from an oak. Some further interpretation may be possible.

In stanza 17 of 'Thyrsis' night falls and "Eve lets down her veil" in the best eighteenth-century style—a vestigial echo of "preferment's door" in the other poem. The poet crosses into another field and hails "the Tree! the Tree!" as a happy omen—

> *Hear it, O Thyrsis, still our tree is there!—*
> *Ah, vain!*

This means in the first place that Clough cannot hear his recognizing cry because he is dead. But it may also mean—"Ah, vain"—that the tree exists only in his imagination and is therefore a token of what he cannot "reach," of what he still wishes might be and knows cannot be. For he also is

> *Still nursing the unconquerable hope,*
> *Still clutching the inviolable shade*

of his faded dreams of devoting his life to poetry. He is still hoping to finish his 'Lucretius,' for example. Just as the Scholar-Gipsy is and is not there, so the tree is and is not there. Arnold had set forth confidently to revisit it, as a twofold symbol of renewing his own youth and of renewing his old associations with Clough. He had almost failed, and then lo, there the tree was—or so he fancied. But it was only a vain imagination. He had not recovered his old sense of admiring friendship, try as he would—"Ah, vain!" Clough certainly was not there and could not hear him say, "still our tree is there!"; and the attempt to recover for himself the enthusiasm of those Oxford days had turned to irony. His first confidence was self-deception, and he recognized this by only pretending he had found the tree. Finally, he underscores the irony by asking of Clough a consoling whisper of renewed hope—

> *Why faintest thou? I wander'd till I died.*
> *Roam on! The light we sought is shining still.*
> *Dost thou ask proof? Our tree yet crowns the hill,*
> *Our Scholar travels yet the loved hill-side.*

Clough had died without fulfilling his early promise. Would Arnold do the same? Was their search for that "fugitive and gracious light" an illusion, like the search for the old Scholar of Glanville's tale?

This interpretation need not be pressed, for it may contain an element of which Arnold was not altogether conscious; but it bears out what nearly every reader has felt, that the lament is less for Clough than for Arnold's own lost ambitions, his nagging regret for the choice he had made in 1851.

9. 'Stanzas from the Grande Chartreuse'

i

FIRST, it is an odd *poème de noces*. But Arnold was not such a romantic as to neglect other considerations. The gay worldling of his Oxford days had chosen a new life. Moreover, he had been for several years meditating a poem on some such subject. His jottings are: "To Meta—the cloister & life liveable"; "religious yearning—an education by a chapel —youth—marriage—children—death   the religious longing never quenched"; "world religion stanzas."

Arnold was married in June 1851 and on the wedding trip stopped at Grenoble on Saturday, 6 September. On Sunday, the seventh, he was at Chambéry. His visit to the monastery was therefore brief; he was not too well informed about its affairs; he seems to have attended Mass without understanding the ritual. But what he saw and heard was enough to provide a setting for ideas and feelings which he brought with him. Though Mrs. Arnold accompanied him, she has no part in the poem.

The introductory narrative is fairly circumstantial. On a rainy, windy evening, the autumn crocuses blooming in the meadow, he set out from St. Laurent-du-Pont, followed the

Guiers Mort upstream, paused where the "mule-track" leaves it, and saw above through the mist La Courerie, turned left and began the last climb, and at the monastery rested and supped in an "outbuilding." Then "Knock; pass the wicket!" and there he is. Stanza by stanza, as though with his guide, he goes through the silent courts, the chapel, the cells, the library, the garden. Then the point of view shifts—"Those halls" (stanza 11) and the important question

—And what am I, that I am here?

It was not a complete tour, but adequate for the purpose.

The introduction is a blend of ornamental narrative, marred only by the absurd rhetoric of

> *Look! through the showery twilight grey*
> *What pointed roofs are these advance?—*
> *A palace of the kings of France?*
>
> *Approach, for what we seek is here!*

and ornamental description, the "stone-carved basins cold" of the fountains, the "ghostlike . . . Cowl'd forms," and so on; and the garden with its "fragrant herbs" from which the famous liqueur is prepared, delicately reported as

> *Of human tasks their only one,*
> *And cheerful works beneath the sun.*

As often with Arnold, there is no transition. The journey recorded and the setting described, Arnold asks a question which the next seventeen stanzas answer: What am I [doing] here *"in this living tomb"?* He replies first: Perhaps I should not be here, "For rigorous teachers" have already purged my earlier religious beliefs and replaced them with [only] the "white star of Truth." He has not forsaken those "masters of the mind"; he is here not as a disciple of the Carthusians, though there is something in common between his situation and theirs; but- –and now the famous simile—but as a Greek might stand before a Runic stone, symbol of the ancient Germanic religion, and think with a sense of pity and awe of his own Gods—

> *For both were faiths, and both are gone.*

This is deceptively simple and must be followed cautiously. The Greek, it should be observed, is not dated: he might be a contemporary, though not necessarily a Christian, thinking of the ancient Greek religion long since "gone," or he might be a Greek of the late fifth or early fourth century B.C. when the old faith of Homeric times had vanished. It makes no difference. Arnold has presented him merely as "a Greek." But now, 1851, Arnold can say and does say only that the two religions, that of the early Germanic peoples and that of the ancient Greeks, are extinct—and here he is in the Grande Chartreuse, which represents to him another religion "gone."

The complexities now begin to weave their tangled skein. The original picture of the thoughtful Greek is abandoned, and the comparison of him and Matthew Arnold, standing likewise in pity and awe in this monastery, is developed somewhat in the manner of a Homeric simile. Not only have the old Greek and Germanic faiths disappeared, but also Arnold's own faith in the religion of his youth—Dr. Arnold's Broad Church of the Anglican Establishment (for which has been substituted the abstract Truth)—*and also* the mediæval faith of St. Bruno, of which the Carthusians are now but a vestigial remnant, "A dead time's exploded dream." This makes four faiths which "are gone."

Arnold now sees himself as hung between two worlds (the Greek and Germanic and mediæval as well as for him the contemporary Anglicanism, which are all four "dead") and the painful present, with a more forlorn future to come. And now two fresh threads are woven in: the world (present and future) and his own melancholy (present and past). This melancholy seems to have nothing to do with his loss of orthodox faith or with his aspirations towards the star of Truth; in terms of the original comparison it displaces them. The world derides his melancholy as it derides the Carthusians, and though he had just denied that he was "their friend" he asks them to shelter him till he can escape from his present constricting circumstances—"chafed by hourly false control" (somewhat as Fausta was "time's chafing prisoner"). The sciolists of the world, he continues, rebuke his melancholy because they have high hopes for the future: they are never "sad!" Arnold does not identify these sciolists—the very name condemns them—but they are the future Roebucks, the new Philistines, the creators of a modern age of "industrial development and social amelioration," "an era of progress" (Preface, 1853). As he had appealed to the Carthusians to shelter him, he now begs the sciolists to leave him and those who share his melancholy—

> Last of the race of them who grieve—

in the silence of the monastery. Silence is all. "The kings of modern thought" have fallen into apathy, whereas "Our fathers," their fathers, were outspoken, their cries were heard everywhere,—but they have left us their sorrows. Who are these fathers? They are Byron and Shelley and Senancour, and they too "are gone." Only the eternal triflers remain, ushering in "an age wanting in moral grandeur."

Thus what began with Arnold's loss of religious faith, as was natural and proper to the monastic background, becomes a lament for "the strange disease of modern life"; what he finds now as discredited, "gone," is the Romantic philosophy of acknowledged melancholy and with it the future of poetry.

Nowadays, "amid the bewildering confusion of our times," reigns the new science with its laws and its triumphs "over time and space." This, he says sarcastically, we can "admire with awe," if only we may be permitted our tears as well. But last of all, with something of Shelley's faith in perfectible man, he brings the Victorian note of confidence in, faintly and with a relaxation of grammar—

> *Years hence, perhaps, may dawn an age*
> *More fortunate, alas! than we—*

just as years later he will have Senancour offer in a vision

> *Hope to a world new-made.*

'Obermann Once More' is a companion piece, a re-echo of these closing reflections in the Grande Chartreuse.

We have come a long way from the "Cowl'd forms" in their "world-famed home" and the thoughtful Greek facing a Runic stone. The two lost faiths became four, the star of Truth was lost sight of, and the world—always a pregnant word for Arnold—first two and then four: a remote past, sanctified by religious faith, a less remote past colored by Romantic melancholy, a distressful present, and an uncertain future—with the poet "Wandering" among them.

With this loud *cri de cœur* Arnold makes himself a spokesman for those whose faith had been undermined by the new spirit of science and religious questioning and who grieve over the loss of what the former age at its best had stood for. This is what used to be called Arnold's *note*. Its tones sound to us a little shrill. For how many besides himself he spoke is an open question; he probably exaggerated—hence the exclamatory rhetoric—his own state. But he made some striking verses out of it, and then softened the tones by his closing simile. We, he says, all we who feel thus, are recluses, like children reared in a simple old faith who hear with poignant distress the noises of the active world about them.

ii

The new picture is almost too much like that of the Grande Chartreuse. The "old-world abbey" surrounded by forests is of course not the monastery he has just visited and described. The last words of the poem, in *Fraser's,* are right: "leave our forest to its peace." When he reprinted the poem in 1867 he altered *forest* to *desert.* Not only does *desert* not fit the surroundings of his "old-world abbey," it is actually the name—Le Déserte: did he not know?—of the district on his left as he followed the Guiers Mort till *"Strike leftward!* cries our guide." This is almost as though to certify, against his own evidence, that he was still thinking of the Grande Chartreuse and he had to declare the fact.

M. Bonnerot has well observed (p. 175) that the closing simile is not a logical conclusion to the poem. The contrast hitherto has been chronological: the failure of past religions, including romanticism, and the failure or promise of failure of the present substitutes. Now Arnold contrasts the two worlds of the active and reclusive life, which is only another form of his own inner conflict, his choice (now made but not now fully accepted) between the 'world' and his 'soul.' What the "children" reply is: Leave us to our secluded life. This aligns them with the Carthusians; but the poet is neither for the Carthusians nor for the children. Can this be after all what he meant to convey, in spite of the overt inconsistency of "no organ" in the monastery and "organ" in the abbey, when he substituted *desert* for *forest* in the last line. What he has done here is what he does also at the end of 'The Scholar-Gipsy,' with the more famous simile of the "grave Tyrian trader" and the "merry Grecian coaster." The equations are correct up to a point—the scholar is to avoid "feverish contact" with our modern life as the serious Tyrian is to avoid the too cheerful Greek with his light freightage. And what is artistically wrong, in both poems, is the introduction, for a final flourish, of pictures admirable in themselves but out of harmony with the tone and feeling of the rest of the poems and disproportionately long, so that they tend to displace the poems themselves in our memory.

iii

The abbey into which the Grande Chartreuse dissolves has been traced by Tinker and Lowry (p. 249) to Chateaubriand's *Génie de Christianisme*, III, v, 2, where Chateaubriand lists the monasteries in the Lebanon, in Egypt, in Panama and the Andes, and ends with the sentence quoted by Tinker and Lowry. But this seems to be the only connection. I do not understand their attribution to Lamartine of the poem which follows chapter 2. Chateaubriand says that it is "un morceau précieux que nous devons à l'amitié. L'auteur y a fait si grands changements, que c'est, pour ainsi dire, un nouvel ouvrage." The poem itself runs to more than two hundred alexandrines. At the beginning the poet says (l. 3):

> *Laisse-moi m'égarer dans ces jardins rustiques,*

and at the end:

> *Quand mon cœur nourrira quelque peine secrète,*
> *Dans ces moments plus doux et si chers au poëte,*
> *Où, fatigué du monde, il veut, libre du moins,*
> *Et jouir de lui-même et rêver sans témoins,*
> *Alors je reviendrai, solitude tranquille,*
> *Oublier dans ton sein les ennuis de la ville*
> *Et retrouver encor [sic] sous ces lambris déserts*
> *Les mêmes sentiments retracés dans ces vers.*

Can there be some confusion with Lamartine's 'Improvisée à la

Grande Chartreuse,' which was no. xxv in *Nouvelles médita-tions poétiques,* Paris, 1823? This is a small poem of eight stanzas. The stars, it says, have their sapphire chariots and the eagle at least his wing, O Lord, but

> *Nous n'avons rien que nos soupirs.*

> *Que la voix de tes saints s'élève et te désarme;*
> *La prière du juste est l'encens des mortels;*
> *Et nous, pécheurs, passons: nous n'avons qu'une larme*
> *A répandre sur tes autels.*

There may be some relation to Arnold's poem, either a parallel or possibly a contributory suggestion for it. But it is certain that when Chateaubriand's *Génie de Christianisme* was pub-lished Lamartine was only twelve years of age.

10. *'Empedocles on Etna'*

A FTER THE eighteen admirable pages in Tinker and Lowry on Arnold's masterpiece, the many observations on it in Professor Bonnerot's large volume, and the elaborate introduction to his translation (Paris, [1947]), there might seem to be little left to glean. I shall therefore add first some notes on the metrical forms as illustrating Arnold's solicitous workmanship in that somewhat neglected field, and as affording a contrast to his perverse misunderstanding of the whole poem. Or if further excuse were needed, one might recall the opinion of T. Sturge Moore, in 1938, that *"Empedocles* more and more appears the most considerable poem of a comparable length by a Victorian."

i

Act I, scene i, starts like a blank verse play on the Elizabethan model, and is short. But scene ii, three times as long, is nearly all lyrical, dominated by the long, gritty Ode delivered by Empedocles, but relieved by the two Songs of Callicles, one of them in blank verse. Nearly two-thirds of Act II is spoken by Empedocles, about evenly divided between blank verse and free verse. The other third comprises three Songs by Callicles. The whole poem runs to 1121 lines, a little less

than one of the shorter Greek tragedies. The Ode and Callicles' five Songs account for more than half. It is obvious,
therefore, that Arnold had neither classical nor modern models
before him, but suited the form to his peculiar needs. This
hybrid form of "dramatic poem" came along with the revived
interest in Elizabethan drama early in the century. Byron and
Shelley in their own ways experimented with it, and Browning
followed. Arnold's use of it, however, differs in being un-
abashedly not a blend but a juxtaposition of the two modes,
drama and poem.

Much of the blank verse is lyrical in tone. The opening
speech of Callicles, a kind of Prologos, begins and ends dramatically:

> *The mules, I think, will not be here this hour. . . .*
>
> > *Who's here?*
>
> *Pausanius! and on foot? alone?*

'Dramatic' also are the exclamatory "O Pan," and "Apollo!"
But there is in between first a lyrico-descriptive nature picture
and then the thematic

> *What mortal could be sick or sorry here? . . .*
> *But if, as most men say, he is half mad*
> *With exile,*

with the romantic note of "a lovelier cure." Pausanius and
Callicles between them review the mental state of Empedocles
and plan to "keep his mind from preying on itself." Pausanius
does this by leaving him to the musical interludes of Callicles;
and Callicles tries but fails. There could hardly be a better
scene i. The tone is clear, the exposition is comprehensive
though brief. Callicles, who is a foil to the hero, serves as a
sort of Chorus and is a good analyst. One major theme is
established: music and the "lovelier cure" of natural beauty

are unable to relax the "settled gloom" of the exiled philosopher. But whatever might deserve the adjective 'lyrical' is remanded by the Ode, which consumes more than half of the act. Empedocles speaks, says the stage direction, "accompanying himself in a solemn manner, on his harp." Yet how the harp could salvage the metrical roughness is beyond imagination. The stanzas—there are seventy[1] and there seem to be more—are a variation of the pattern which Shelley used for his 'Skylark' and which Swinburne, with a further variation, later forced into music for 'Hertha.' They go in pairs $abab^3c^6$, the following stanza having the matching c-rime.[2] (Swinburne adopted a similar device with the Omar quatrain in his 'Laus Veneris.') The scheme was not unpromising, but the condensed phrasing and the hard unpoetic style defeat its possibilities. The best that can be said is that Empedocles was wrestling with self-expression and his thought was both cabined, cribbed, confined, and far from lucid. He calls it later his "lesson" to Pausanias. It is an omnium gatherum of classical and modern ideas (some of them rather like the coda of 'Resignation'). Following a "long pause" Callicles sings of Cadmus and Harmonia, who after "all that Theban woe" are transformed into serpents, "Placid and dumb"; and Empedocles, dismissing Pausanias, "departs on his way up the mountain."

Act II is a long soliloquy of Empedocles before the suicidal plunge, broken by two Songs of Callicles, heard from below through the "loud noise" of the erupting volcano. First

[1] Tinker and Lowry print two more (p. 292) which Arnold omitted and fragments of three others (p. 293) among Arnold's notes for his Lucretius—which suggests that already in 1852 he was making thrifty use here of verses that were later to be transferred to his long planned and never accomplished *chef d'œuvre*.

[2] As an extra flourish the rimes *ours* : *powers* (ll. 221, 226) are repeated in inverse order after two intervening stanzas: *powers* : *ours* (ll. 241, 246).

Callicles sings in praise of music, telling the ancient story of the rebel Typho buried beneath the mountain; and then Empedocles adds the moral:

The brave impetuous heart [Typho] *yields everywhere*
To the subtle, contriving head [Zeus].

The meter of the Song is balanced like strophe and antistrophe: two quatrains followed by two groups of twenty lines matching both in rime scheme and line length. The quatrains go abb^5a^3, save that the first b line is varied to a different tune—

In the court of gods, in the city of men.

The two longer sections are more complex, but each closely matches the other, like strophe and antistrophe, each consisting of first a group of seven lines, then two groups of six lines, followed by a closing triplet. The two seven-line groups have identical patterns: $abcdabd^4$. The first six-line groups have also identical patterns: $a^4ba^5c^4b^3c^5$, but here the strophe has a wholly new set of rimes, whereas in the antistrophe the c-rime repeats the c-rime of the preceding seven-line group—thus leaving the c-rime of the strophe's seven-line group without an answer. The second groups of six lines are also identical in pattern (which however differs from that of the first six-line groups) and again have all new rimes: $a^4bca^5cb^4$. The triplets are also identical in pattern: a^4aa^5.—All this may be expressed perhaps more simply. Both strophe and antistrophe have four groups or stanzas, composed of seven, six, six, three lines respectively, and each of these stanzas matches its corresponding stanza in rime scheme and line length. Strophe and antistrophe differ in two respects: (1) in the strophe the c-rime of the first stanza has no answer, whereas in the antistrophe it is answered by the c-rime of the second stanza; and (2) there is no pause at the end of the second stanza of the antistrophe corresponding to that in the strophe.

The diligence required to achieve this resemblance to a Greek choric ode is surely worth special recognition.

The next Song of Callicles is also in praise of music, now telling the story of Apollo and Marsyas. The moral needs no pointing: Empedocles simply puts off his laurel, "Scornful Apollo's ensign." It begins, like the preceding Song, with two quatrains, but of a different pattern: $a^5b^3a^5b^3$ and $a^4b^5a^4b^5$. Then come thirty-six 4-stress trochaic lines, at first in couplets, then with rimes irregularly placed (between two of them there are nine intervening lines, between two others twelve) but ending with a couplet; then twenty-six similarly trochaic lines beginning with couplets and ending with a couplet whose last line is drawn out:

> *Ah, poor Faun, poor Faun! ah, poor Faun!*

The rimes are unexceptional but for *trees : villages* and *born : Faun, scorn : Faun;* and also *sing : playing,* which has historical precedent but is usually associated with the Pre-Raphaelite mode.

Little of the blank verse is distinctive. Some of it is heavy and awkward, some smooth and easy, with here and there a hint of Keats and of the early Tennysonian music. There are a few striking 'irregularities':

> *Thou wilt earn my thanks sure, and perhaps his . . .*
> *The sweetest harp-player in Catana . . .*
> *And the world hath the day, and must break thee.*

It is in the soliloquies of Empedocles in Act II that the interesting combinations of blank verse and free verse occur.

> *He fables, yet speaks truth!*
> *The brave, impetuous heart yields everywhere*
> *To the subtle, contriving head;*
> *Great qualities are trodden down,*
> *And littleness united*
> *Is become invincible.*

These rumblings are not Typho's groans, I know!
These angry smoke-bursts
Are not the passionate breath
Of the mountain-crush'd, tortur'd, intractable Titan king—

and so on. The Old Testament sounds in

Thou keepest aloof the profane,
But the solitude oppresses thy votary!
The jars of men reach him not in thy valley—
But can life reach him?
Thou fencest him from the multitude—
Who will fence him from himself?
He hears nothing but the cry of the torrents,
And the beating of his own heart.

There is a Wordsworthian power, as well as Wordsworthian
flatness, in

Then we could still enjoy, then neither thought
Nor outward things were clos'd and dead to us;
But we receiv'd the shock of mighty thoughts
On simple minds with a pure natural joy;
And if the sacred load oppress'd our brain,
We had the power to feel the pressure eased,
The brow unbound, the thoughts flow free again,
In the delightful commerce of the world.
We had not lost our balance then, nor grown
Thought's slaves, and dead to every natural joy.
The smallest thing could give us pleasure then—

And this is immediately followed by a descending and ascending series of short lines: first a line of three full stresses, then
three lines which hover between three and two stresses, then
a line of two stresses only, and then stepped up to a line which
again hovers between two and three stresses, and finally one
with three full stresses, matching the first:

> *The sports of the country-people,*
> *A flute-note from the woods,*
> *Sunset over the sea;*
> *Seed-time and harvest,*
> *The reapers in the corn,*
> *The vinedresser in his vineyard,*
> *The village-girl at her wheel!*[3]

A little after this there is an ascending series of 2-, 3-, 3/4-, 4-stress lines followed by six lines graduating upwards from the line with four stresses on four syllables to the dactylic 5-stress line with fourteen syllables.

> *And you, ye stars,*
> *Who slowly begin to marshal,*
> *As of old, in the fields of heaven,*
> *Your distant, melancholy lines!*
> *Have you, too, survived yourselves?*
> *Are you, too, what I fear to become?*
> *You, too, once lived;*
> *You, too, moved joyfully*
> *Among august companions,*
> *In an older world, peopled by Gods,*
> *In a mightier order,*
> *The radiant, rejoicing, intelligent Sons of Heaven.*

The peak of dramatic eloquence, accompanied by a verse movement of equal strength, comes in Empedocles' following address to the stars:

> *—the sea of cloud,*
> *That heaves its white and billowy vapours up*
> *To moat this isle of ashes from the world,*
> *Lives; and that other fainter sea, far down,*
> *O'er whose lit floor a road of moonbeams leads*
> *To Etna's Liparëan sister-fires*
> *And the long dusky line of Italy—*

[3] There is a similar tapering near the end of the poem, ll. 399-402, where the stresses are four, four, three, three, three and the syllable count eight, seven, seven, five, four.

> *That mild and luminous floor of waters lives,*
> *With held-in joy swelling its heart; I only,*
> *Whose spring of hope is dried, whose spirit has fail'd—*
> *I, who have not, like these, in solitude*
> *Maintain'd courage and force, and in myself*
> *Nursed an immortal vigour—I alone*
> *Am dead to life and joy; therefore I read*
> *In all things my own deadness.*

The feeling of blank verse dwindles almost to that of free verse, while its form remains; then the last incomplete line certifies the gradual change of movement.

After Empedocles leaps into the crater Callicles sings, still "from below," the exodos or epilogue or palinode—one hardly knows what. As the volcano erupts he says this is no place for Apollo and the Muses, yet he sees them ascending Olympus, praising the All-Father

>   *and then,*
> *The rest of immortals,*
> *The action of men.*
>
> *The day in his hotness,*
> *The strife with the palm;*
> *The night in her silence,*
> *The stars in their calm.*

Musically it is a benediction, dramatically a confusion, but metrically a curious masterpiece. It consists of thirteen stanzas *abcb*². The closing lines, just quoted, show the formal pattern: iamb and anapest. What is notable is that this apparently rollicking meter is so managed that through the first seven stanzas, or until Apollo is seen, nearly every line has some extra weight (iamb or anapest given a spondaic increment), with the resultant effect that while Callicles is saying that Apollo should not be here

> *The line too labours and the words move slow.*

Then for the last six stanzas the movement is lighter, swifter, more even and smoother. Callicles begins:

> *Through the black, rushing smoke-bursts,*
> *Thick breaks the red flame;*
> *All Etna heaves fiercely*
> *Her forest-cloth'd frame.*
>
> *Not here, O Apollo!*
> *Are haunts meet for thee,*
> *But, where Helicon breaks down*
> *In cliff to the sea.*

Compare these stanzas with the last two: can anyone doubt the conscious planning and secure execution?

The bravura show-piece of all, however, is Callicles' first song, called by Arnold 'The Last Glen' in 1855 (when he reprinted from 'Empedocles' only this and the later song of Callicles on Cadmus and Harmonia). It is in two parts, a pictorial introduction for the setting, which belongs partly in the idyl tradition of Theocritus and Landor and the Small Sweet one of *The Princess,* and metrically in the 'Lycidas' tradition; and second, twenty ordinary four-stress iambic lines telling of the old Centaur Chiron and the young Achilles. The simple movement of this is varied midway by a cunning parallelism: abab:

> *And where the soaking springs abound,*
> *And the straight ashes grow for spears,*
> *And where the hill-goats come to feed,*
> *And the sea-eagles build their nest.*

The opening section abounds in subtleties, some of which belong as much to prose rhythm as to meter.

> *The track winds down to the clear stream,*
> *To cross the sparkling shallows; there*
> *The cattle love to gather, on their way*

To the high mountain-pastures, and to stay,
Till the rough cow-herds drive them past,
Knee-deep in the cool ford; for 'tis the last
Of all the woody, high, well-water'd dells
On Etna; and the beam
Of noon is broken there by chestnut-boughs
Down its steep verdant sides; the air
Is freshen'd by the leaping stream, which throws
Eternal showers of spray on the moss'd roots
Of trees, and veins of turf, and long dark shoots
Of ivy-plants, and fragrant hanging bells
Of hyacinths, and on late anemonies,
That muffle its wet banks; but glade,
And stream, and sward, and chestnut trees,
End here; Etna beyond, in the broad glare
Of the hot noon, without a shade,
Slope behind slope, up to the peak, lies bare;
The peak, round which the white clouds play.

Note first that for a rime to *play* the ear goes back seventeen
lines, and then is greeted by the opening line of the second
section:

In such a glen, on such a day. . . .

The spondaic tendency is announced in the very first line:
winds down and *clear stream*, followed at once by the lilt of
To cross the sparking shallows, itself echoed in *The cattle love
to gather*. The third and fourth lines end almost alike, with
quasi-anapests; but the effects are entirely different. In the
sixth line, which would naturally run to five iambs, the
spondaic movement returns with *knee-deep, cool ford*, and is
repeated in *steep ver-, moss'd roots, wet banks, broad glare,
hot noon, lies bare;* and these are still further emphasized by
three adjacent stresses in *high, well-wa-, long dark shoots,
-trees End here, peak lies bare*, and the final *white clouds play.*
And all these variations are of course accommodated to the

normal expected iambic flow. To them must be added the choriambic effect of *Etna beyond, Slope beyond slope, up to the peak,* and (less noticeable) *round which the white. In the broad glare* is repeated in *Of the hot noon.* Thus the whole becomes a kind of chant or recitative introducing the aria which follows, and combines with metrical subtleties, subtleties borrowed from the rhythm of prose. No one writes like this without a trained ear and without meticulous attention to prosodic detail; and Arnold, who used to be accused of having no musical sense, should have the highest praise for this display.

ii

These metrical analyses make dull reading but they may be justified as evidence, often missed, of Arnold's attention to prosody in his valiant effort to make his 'Empedocles' as fine a work as possible. The more wonder, therefore, that he went so far astray in the general conception of his poem and most of all in his explanation of it. Certainly he had gone a long way from his original plan to represent a "refusal of limitation by the religious sentiment." He seems dead set to prove Tallyrand's epigram: "Si nous nous explicons nous cesserons de nous entendre."

In his Preface, 1853, Arnold tried to explain why he was dissatisfied with his poem.[4] He felt it was successful in delineating "the feeling of one of the last Greek religious philosophers," who was out of harmony with his times and who lived into an age of Sophists when "the dialogue of the mind with itself" had set in, when "the doubts" and "the discouragement, of Hamlet and of Faust," prevailed. "In such situations there is inevitably something morbid, in the description of them

[4] For valuable comment on this "exasperating" Preface, and also on 'Empedocles,' see Frank Kermode, *Romantic Image,* London, [1957], pp. 12-19.

something monotonous. When they occur in actual life they are painful, not tragic; the representation of them in poetry is painful also." (So much for the masterpieces of Shakespeare and of Goethe. Arnold did not however, like Tennyson only a few years later, expose himself by calling 'Empedocles' a "little Hamlet.") Moreover, his "the representation of them in poetry is painful also" is a somewhat off-hand deliverance on a matter for which Aristotle and many others after him have sought a solution. It was Arnold's business as poet to make the situation of Empedocles not painful to the reader, for therein lies the difference between life and the "criticism of life." And since he succeeded in making it not painful, the grounds for his dissatisfaction must lie elsewhere.

The subject, he thought, was too modern; it had none of the "exclusive characteristics," "the calm, the cheerfulness, the disinterested objectivity" of "the great monuments of early Greek genius." (Did he regard the great Greek tragedies as cheerful?) In a word, neither the subject nor his treatment of it was sufficiently like a poem of Sophocles; and in this of course Arnold was right. But he was apparently irked by Ludlow's assertion, in the *North British Review* for August 1853, at the very moment he was writing his Preface, that "A true allegory of the state of one's own mind in a representative history is perhaps the highest thing that one can attempt in the way of poetry," and therefore he had to defend his choice of an ancient subject; apparently also he was even more annoyed by the remarks of Shairp and others that he had put too much of himself into his poem, had "used it for the drapery of his own thoughts." Fifteen years later he returned to the defense on this point in the letter to Dunn quoted by Tinker and Lowry, pp. 287-88. And all this led to certain confusions.

For his poem he had read up on Empedocles and the pre-Socratic philosophers, and he contrived to get a great deal of his 'sources,' ancient and modern, into the text. He could honestly assert to Dunn that his own creed was not then or later "by any means identical with" that of Empedocles, though he felt "a sympathy with the figure Empedocles presents to the imagination." But there was no need to deplore the notion that he had used Empedocles as a mouthpiece for some of his own opinions. For it was legitimate to create out of the fragmentary remains an imaginary Empedocles and it was legitimate to put as much of himself as he liked into his only semihistorical figure of the Greek religious philosopher. That he should have failed to recognize this is interesting; that he chose to include the legend of the suicidal leap into the volcano is possibly significant, apart from the obvious 'drama.' Possibly he thought of himself as committing a kind of suicide when he sacrificed his poetic ambitions for the sake of "the world" of security, marriage, and school inspecting; what in the same volume he called

> *the gradual furnace of the world,*
> *In whose hot air our spirits are upcurl'd*
> *Until they crumble, or else grow like steel—*
> *Which kills in us the bloom, the youth, the spring.*

Possibly it was this that led him to project some of his predicament into that of Empedocles, and to regret the public confession.

Yet what Arnold was most unable to see is that the failure of his "Dramatic Poem," its failure to satisfy him, was due less to the morbidity or painfulness of the subject than to his undramatic handling of it.[5] It was not so much the lack of

[5] In his 1853 Preface Arnold lists "the situations" from which "no poetical enjoyment can be derived"; namely, "those in which the suffering finds no vent in action; in which a continuous state of mental distress is prolonged, unrelieved by incident, hope, or resistence; in which there is everything to be endured, nothing to be done." These situations are really one; the list seems to have been composed to fit his

"disinterested objectivity" as the lack of a total conception of the theme as tragic that betrayed him. Instead of a "representation" of his protagonist wrestling with the causes of his despair and being driven by them to his final act, Arnold gives us only the "settled gloom," the overwrought emotional state of Empedocles immediately before he leaps into the crater. He gives us no dramatic action, intellectual or emotional, leading to the catastrophe. The Songs of Callicles serve only to intensify the despondency of Empedocles, not to determine the outcome. His decision is already made at the end of Act I when he says, "Farewell, Pausanius," and is foreseen by Callicles in his third speech; for Callicles then hopes only to "soothe him," not to prevent the catastrophe. Nor is the catastrophe entirely clear. After his proud boast,

> *Yea, I take myself to witness,*
> *That I have loved no darkness,*
> *Sophisticated no truth,*
> *Nursed no delusion,*
> *Allow'd no fear!*

Empedocles feels a sense of exaltation as he leaps into the "sea of fire." He cries:

> *My soul glows to meet you. . . .*
> *Receive me! save me!*

Despair and purification are mingled. He will return to the world,

---

own "Empedocles, as I have endeavoured to represent him." Therefore, he says justly, he has excluded the poem from his New Edition of 1853, as being "poetically faulty." He does not plead the final suicide as "action," but what he would not recognize is the difference between poetically and dramatically faulty. He provides no action or plot in the Aristotelian sense, no series of incidents or cumulative situations which produce a catastrophe,—hardly even a graduated series of intensified emotional states.

Go through the sad probation all again,

with still the faint hope that he will conquer not only *sense* but also his present slavery to *thought*. Suicide is a form of salvation. (This resembles what happened to Mycerinus, and may contain also a personal 'allegory.')

Thus the skill and effort which Arnold devoted to parts of his plan—"I intended to delineate"—make all the more ironic his disappointment with the result. But he had planned also something "Greek" and it turned out something different, but something equally or almost equally good, though he was unwilling to admit it in his Preface. He was unwilling to admit it because of his preoccupation, at the moment, with ancient *vs.* modern subjects and of his sensitiveness over a sort of self-revelation. But now we at least can see it as what it is, a study in morbidity and an admirable one, comparable with Tennyson's much later treatment of Lucretius (1864)— which must have horrified him. And as an allegory of the state of his own mind it was no doubt a powerful catharsis.

Index